AF231070

ANTHEM
OF HOPE

Dean C Gardner

Contents

Dedicated to the memory
of my second wife.

SECTION 1:
Through the looking glass

In the center
Of being and nothingness
Cosmic consciousness
Worked the mystery of life
As meditation stirred
Pure music
Into being toward Truth.

There was
The pounding in the heart
Of the drums of eternity
And visions surfaced
In her third eye.

From across a sky
Of flames
A lone crow
Delivered manna
From The Unknown God
And Annabelle Lee walked
Through the walls of death.

Then
Trumpets sounded
And the crow
Opened a portal
To the beyond.

Then
Time dissolved into a pool of fire.

How
The moment took
Her into the other side
Of what was there
And she saw the destiny
Of the power mongers.

Then
Her vision took her
To a mountain of glory
That issued the picture
Of the always already there
And the drums of eternity
Brought her a new life.

Time and times
And a half unfolded
When the children of promise
Formed a choir of patriots
And they were armed
With the artillery
Of forevermore.

So
Annabelle Lee stepped
Back into life
With the faith
In what matters
And cosmic consciousness
Embraced her
With the love
Of The Unknown God.

*

So
The Word is there
To teach the way
The Truth and the life
Through the looking glass
Of the always already there
As Eagle Hawk traveled
Into the unknown.

Stepping outside
Of time and space
He configured himself
As a witness to Truth
A pilgrim on a journey
Into the mystery of life.

As Eagle Hawk entered
Meditation
Time and times and a half
Dissolved into pure music
And the sound
Of the deep touch
Filled him
with blessed assurance.

Then
The dull round eclipsed
Being toward Truth
And darkness fell
Upon his heart.

It was
The movement of possibility
That staggered him
With being and nothingness
As he advanced
Into the dwelling
Of the authentic article.

So
Wounded
By phenomenal reality
He leaned on The Word
And he became
A vision
Of what mattered.

How
Eternity was the beginning
Of the given.

How
The substance of life
Fed him with the deep touch.

How
Mind fashioned
Being toward Truth with promise.

Then
Eagle Hawk dwelt in pure music.

*

It was
Through her third eye
That she found a way
Through the dull round
Onto the everlasting
As the no longer

Shadowed times
and a half.

It was
Being toward death
That awakened her
To the other side
Of time and space
Where pure music
emanated life
into forevermore.

Although
The will to be
Triumphed
Over the darkness
Of nothingness
Self-deception
Weighed upon her heart.

Then
The kiss of cosmic consciousness
Delivered mind into the dynamic
Of the always already there
As Annabelle Lee took
To the wind
Of a parabola of time.

Then
The image
Of what matters
Gathered in the moment
When Lady Liberty embraced
The freedom of being toward Truth.

Then
Time and space
Coincided with the struggle
To be
While the vision
Of deliverance cleansed
The heart.

So
The unknown called
The mind to Truth
Envisioning purpose
As the life
Of Lady Liberty.

*

So
It was war and Lady Liberty
Took her stand
As Eagle Hawk covered her back.

How
Brutal the war
In mind and heart
When times and a half
Shred being toward Truth.

So
The cities burn
And the flesh writhes
In pain.

Then
Lady Liberty called
The need
To serve and protect
And Eagle Hawk
Gave himself
As present
And accounted for.

There was
A troupe of patriots
Configured
As lock and load
And they readied their gear
To face the conflict.

As they advanced
To the front lines
The domestic terrorist
Trembled.

Then
The blood
Of the cancel culture
Painted the streets red.

How
The war
within mind raged
In the gut
Of the here and now
As the troupe
Fired at will.

So
The domestic terrorists
Tried to tread
Upon the land
Of the free and brave.

Then
The destiny
Of Lady Liberty
Secured time
And times and a half
In the hearts and minds
Of the children of promise.

*

Then
There was light
And another day
Dawned from darkness
As the patriots assembled
In the garden
Of tables and chairs.

There was
The movement of spirits
Into the presence
Of being toward Truth
And they loaded destiny
In both barrels.

How
Destiny rubbed
The puppet masters
The wrong way
Giving them
Unmarked graves
In the swamp
Of the no longer
While the patriots
Carried on.

At Eagle Hawk's table
Sat two angels
And Lady Liberty
While he checked
The perimeter

Of being and nothingness
Through meditation.

Time future rolled
Into time present
As Lady Liberty configured
The defense
Of the children of promise
And the angels guided
Her to certain victory.

So
Mind traveled
Through time and space
To the edge of nothingness
Beholding the body
Of the domestic terrorists
For what it was.

Coming out of trance
Eagle Hawk mounted
The here and now
With the conviction
Of cosmic consciousness
Fortifying him
With immutable Truth.

Equipped with the way
The Truth and the life
His courage knew
No limits.

So
It was freedom
That he defended.

*

Long ago
Before the rise
Of the cancel culture
Eagle Hawk frequented
The presence of Annabelle Lee
Because she was a marvel
Above time and space.

Together
They roamed through the land
Of the free and brave
Leaving Truth
As their legacy
As being toward Truth
Embraced cosmic consciousness.

How
Mind travels through trance
Into the unknown
With a heart

As true as pure music
And the wilderness
Of thought shelters
What matters
With the authentic article.

To be
With the light
Of the everlasting
Allows heart
To feel blessed assurance
As trumpets sound
The beginning of eternity.

Because
Back in time past
Annabelle Lee danced
Upon his mind
Freedom sang a battle hymn
In stars and stripes
And destiny pictured
The triumph of love.

How
The deep touch
Moved Eagle Hawk
Onto the beyond
Taking his trance
Into the always
Already there
As The Unknown God
Allowed them
The breath of love.

Then
They dressed
What was there
With endless possibility
As they lived
The life of freedom
The life of love
Forevermore.

*

As mind penetrates
The unknown
Through meditation
Time and times
And a half dissolve
Into a moment
When thought reaches
Being toward Truth
With blessed assurance.

There is
The trumpeting
Of the everlasting
In the heart
As visions stir
With what matters.

There is
The deep touch
Of cosmic consciousness
As pure music unveils
The mystery of life
And images take mind
Beyond being and nothingness.

Overpowering
The drift of mind
These images speak
The language
Of forevermore
Through the authentic article
As thought unearths
Times and a half
Until the peace
Beyond understanding
Dwells in the moment.

Then
Being toward Truth
Speaks the authentic article
In form and substance.

Then
Truth tells of the way
And the life of The Word.

Suddenly
Possibility speaks
To the heart
And the third eye
Configures
Mind intro the close
At hand.

So
Being toward Truth listens
To the song
Of the everlasting
As want and need
Feed upon the manna
From The Unknown God.

*

The drums of eternity
Are pounding life
Into the moment
As cosmic consciousness
Sweeps across the here and now
As time future awakens
Need and want
To the fruits of labor.

It is
The power of meditation
That feels the muscles
Of pure music
As mind lifts the dull round
From hidden meaning.

Then
The mechanism
Of being toward Truth
Constructs a bridge
From time present
To the always already there
And visions picture
The mystery of life
As a two-dimensional
Reality.

In this moment
Heart drifts
In blessed assurance
As the drums of eternity
Roll being and nothingness
Into endless possibility
Into the authentic article.

So
Eagle Hawk erases
The puppet masters
From what is there
And the comrades
Disappear.

There is the quiet
Of the peace beyond
Understanding
That equips
The children of promise
With the deep touch
While Lady Liberty strikes
Truth into the here and now.

Then
The patriots march
Into battle.

Then
The children of promise
Dance in freedom.

So
The trance pictured
The Unknown God
Liberating life
Through a one-dimensional
Reality
Into the hands of The Word.

*

With his mind in chains
And his heart in bondage
All he knew
And all he felt
Was the dark chill
Of nothingness.

To be
A prisoner in the bowels
Of despair he groveled
In an unmarked grave.

There was
The scent of dread
Encompassing
The here and now
As he pulled himself
Into existence.

So this
Was his life day after day.

He could not see
The dawn of freedom.

He could not see
An end to his torment.

Then
The warm light
Of The Word
Came upon him
Taking him
Into the peace
Beyond understanding.

Then
The Unknown God
Freed him
From his bondage
And the chains
Of his torment
Dropped away.

It was
That a day had dawned
When he was given faith
And he accepted
The grace of deliverance.

The years
Of his torment ended
And he was acquitted
Of the guilt in his life.

So
Through faith in The Word
He was reborn
As a child of promise.

*

Digging in the earth
Of being and nothingness
Searching for the way
Of Truth and life
He thought he
Buried the past
In an unmarked grave
But thoughts lingered
In the shadows of mind.

To escape from the blood
On his hands
He washed them
Over and over again
But the spots
Did not go away.

The deaths he caused
Haunted him.

In his life
There was bad blood
And his memories
Of time past
Tormented him.

So
He lived with his guilt
Strangling his life
Tortured
By what he had done.

So
He lived in darkness
Chilled by the blood
That he had loosed.

So
In his mind
A war of principalities raged
And he was losing.

Then
A dawn of light
Cam to him
And the voice
Of cosmic consciousness
Purified his heart.

It was
The song of pure music
Echoing through mind.

It was
The grace of The Unknown God
That delivered him
To the peace beyond
Understanding.

So
By trusting The Word
His faith carried him
Into the wonder
Of living forevermore.

His torment died.

*

So
The domestic terrorists
Came to town
To burn the city down
And it was time
To lock and load.

If the blue lives
Could not rid
This infestation
The patriots backed
By the children of promise
Would strike and strike hard.

This city
Was the home
Of the free and brave
And they would not
Tolerate destruction
Of their homestead.

These were
The days of warmth
And the nights so cool
That brought the appearance
Of autumn
Upon the mountains
As each household
Cleaned their weapons.

To defend
What was theirs
The patriots were ready.

In the garden
Of tables and chairs
Headquarters for the patriots
Lady Liberty listened to the reports
On the activities
Of the domestic terrorists
And Eagle Hawk drew up
Plans for defense.

Time and times
And a half passed

And the blue lives
Took their stand
As the terrorists
Acted up a bit
But the city did not burn.

Looking on
The patriots made
Their presence known.

It was
Obvious to the terrorists
That this town
Would not tolerate
The burning
Of their precious jewel
The homes
Of the free and brave.

So
The domestic terrorists slinked away.

*

In a valley of Tennessee
Known as a mystery
Of life
Eagle Hawk rose
Into trance
As dawn painted
Splendor
Across the mountains.

He saw images
Beyond the possible
That pulled him
Into the deep touch
Infusing his mined
With the celebration
Of The Unknown God
Although the pit
Of no return drew near.

Then
Time and space opened
His third eye
To visions of pure mu8sic
And he was granted life
Day by day one day
At a time.

So
A great affliction
Infected the land
Of the star
Spangled banner
A virus from the East.

It was
A devastating plague
That buried a multitude
In an agonizing death.

How
Cruel this pandemic.

So
Lady Liberty faced this evil
With knowledge and skill
Developing a vaccine
That could counter this virus.

Time and times and a half
Passed
As this evil devoured
The living.

It was
Lady Liberty against
The work
Of the puppet masters.

It was
The will of the patriots
And the prayers
Of the children of promise
That would conquer
This evil.

*

Wandering through
The mystery of life
Following the message
Written in the stars
Eagle Hawk surveyed
The domain of hidden meaning
As the unknown signaled
Another presence
Of the deep touch.

It was
The explosion
Of times and a half
That brought form and substance
To an image
Surfacing in the moment.

Then
Mind figured the calculus
Of being and nothingness
As cosmic consciousness
Revealed the other side
Of time and space.

Leaving the logic
Of the dull round
Eagle Hawk advanced
To the rubric
Of the always already there
As the blood
Of blessed assurance redeemed
All his past.

Then
Eagle Hawk took to the wind
As the deep touch filled him
With the authentic article.

In that moment
Truth took his trance
Into the dwelling
Of The Unknown God
And Lady Liberty appeared
In his mind
Pointing to the way
The Truth and the life.

Then
She placed pure music
In his heart
And he became the metaphor
Of cosmic consciousness.

So
He felt the grace
Of The Unknown God.

*

At daybreak
The clouds covered
The mountains
As a slow rain defined
Time and space.

There was
Blood in the streets
Where domestic terrorists
Ripped life
From the breath
Of being toward Truth
And lifeless bodies defined
The moment.

How
Hollow the rhetoric
Of the puppet masters.

How
Cruel the work
Of the power mongers.

So
The thought-police
Carved minds
Of freedom
Into shreds of dread
And the children of promise
Dropped into despair.

So
Lady Liberty rose
In the midst
Of battle
Upholding Truth
And freedom
And Eagle Hawk struck
The heart of chaos.

There was
The song of pure music
Trumpeting the blood
Of life
Into the celebration
Of victory
After the patriots
Ended the puppet masters
Domain.

So
Cosmic consciousness
Endured the times
Feeding the children
Of promise
With the manna
Of The Unknown God
And The Word
Returned the life of hope
Upon the mindscape.

Then
The dawn of forevermore
Removed the shroud
Of clouds.

*

In the mountains
The wilderness speaks Truth
Into being toward Truth
As rolling thunder
Echoes through the mind
And the heart pounds life
Into the living moment.

In the reaches
Of trance
Possibility surrounds
Time present and visions
Of cosmic consciousness
Picture the splendor
Of forevermore.

So
The deep touch
Of times and a half
Takes thought
Into a portal
To the beyond
And the wilderness
Flourishes
In the bones
Revealing the mystery
Of life.

How
Meditating on the works
Of The Word
Allows mind to visit
What matters most
As trance
Carries thought
Into a parabola of time.

Then
The outback of mind
Fills with visions
As the manna
From The Unknown God
Enriches the experiential.

Leaping outside self
Allows eternity
To turn the moment
Into the always
Already there
As being toward Truth
Thrives in being
In the world
But not of the world.

So
Written upon the heart
Is deliverance
From the dull round
And admittance
Into a wilderness
Of beauty
A garden of joy
Forevermore.

*

Although
Black lives matter started
As an honorable effort
Bringing equality for all
American lives
The domestic terrorists
Corrupted what was there
Into a hate movement
A force determined
To destroy Lady Liberty.

Although
The cancel culture
Brought chaos
Upon the land
Of the free and brave
The children of promise
Took their stand
And the patriots
Fought the good fight.

How
The cities burned
During the riots of 2020
As a testament
To their corrupt ways.

So
Annabelle Lee gathered
Blue lives matter
And all the patriots
As a deterrent
To the killing of Lady Liberty.

Then
She led Truth
Across the nation
With a sword in her right hand
And a dagger in her left.

Wearing the full armor
Of The Unknown God
She mounted the destiny
Of freedom
And led the battle
Of this side
Of the war of principalities.

Ten thousand, thousand angels
Rose across the land
Led by Lady Liberty
As a formidable force
Of Truth and justice.

So
It was the power
Of a more perfect union
That faced hate groups

And the history
Of stars and stripes
Would not be canceled.

*

Rocketing into the deep
Of trance
Eagle Hawk felt
The movement of his earth
Into pure music
As time became times
And a half.

There was
The deep touch of the unknown
Throughout being toward Truth
As he witnessed
The way, the Truth
And the life
And his meditation parted
The sky
Leaving the authentic article
In the opening.

Then
Hidden meaning wrote
The mystery of life
In the blood
Of what matters.

Then
Structure molded substance
Into a clear mind
And eternity appeared
In a hand breath.

Although
He faced the always
Already there
With the look of hope
The dull round
Left traces of the unknown
Upon his countenance.

Then
Time past blasted
Across the moment
With the life
Of despair overshadowing
Time present
But time future
Opened the door
To redemption.

In his trance
Eagle Hawk walked
Through the walls
Of the other side
Of death
As The Unknown God
Spirited him into the peace
Beyond understanding.

Awakening to the here
And now
Eagle Hawk lifted
His eyes to destiny
And blessed assurance
Warmed his heart.

*

SECTION 2:
After time and space

Climbing into the back
Of mind
Grandpa Time set the expanse
Into an order of things
And things in themselves
By the direction
Of The Unknown God.

The hands of eternity
Molded what was there
According to discreet laws
As the physics
Of being and nothingness
Configured time and space.

Then
Being toward Truth appeared
With the breath
From cosmic consciousness
And thoughts probed
The actual.

So
The workings of mind
Could imagine the imp0ossible
In a universe
Of endless possibility.

How
Structure determined
The existence of substance.

All of what was there
Conformed to the rubric
Of being and time.

Then
Grandpa Time numbered
The dimensions of the actual
And there were only three.

Then
Grandpa Time numbered
The presence of time
And there were only three
Time past, time present
And time future
But there also was linear time
A parabola of time
And cosmic time.

Linear time was
A three-dimensional reality.

A parabola of time
Was a two-dimensional reality.

Cosmic time
Was a one-dimensional reality.

So
Eternity moved the heart
Of Grandpa Time
To witness the makings
Of all and everything,

*

As trance takes
Eagle Hawk into the unknown
Visions stir
Toward the open graves
Of times and a half
And a light shines
Upon the way to Truth and life.

There is
The penetration of pure music
Into mind
That liberates
The substance of being toward Truth
And the drums of eternity
Pound a message
From the other side of life.

Reading between the lines
Of what is there
Eagle Hawk probes
The mystery of life
As The Unknown God
Writes upon his heart
With the blood of destiny.

In the shadows
Of the moment
The breath of time past
Shatters his thoughts.

Then
A portal to the beyond
Takes him
To the mercy seat
And he savagely weeps
For deliverance.

Rearranging his life
He drops his folly
Into a chasm
Of the no longer
And he looks to The Word
With hope.

How
He feels the deep touch
Of always and forever.

Then
The Unknown God allows him
To awaken from the dead.

So
He walks through the wall
Of death
To enter the living moment
With a clear mind
And a pure heart.

*

Upon the edge
Of times and a half
Pure music fills the moment
With the deep touch
As the drums of eternity
Move mind
Into the mystery of life.

So
Meditation pyramids thought
Into the unknown
Where the always already there
Pictures the body of Truth.

Gathering understanding
Being toward Truth walks
Through the wall of death
As a portal to forevermore
Opens the third eye
To blessed assurance.

So
Thought sees hidden meaning
In the shadows
Of being and nothingness
As mind contrives
What matters
Out of meaninglessness.

Then
Pure music falls into silence.

Then
The deep touch departs without a trace.

Then
The drums of eternity cease
Leaving dust in the mouth
Of being toward Truth.

Then
The mystery of life confounds understanding.

Then
The Unknown God reaches
Into heart
With the vision of forevermore
As the blood of life wets the earth.

To dwell
In the terrain of possibility
How
The thunder
Of the authentic article
Awakens the heart
To the way, the Truth
And the life.

Then
The Unknown God
Writes blessed assurance
Between the lines
Of being and nothingness
And mind travels
To the other side
Of time and space.

So
It is faith in The Word
That allows mind to grasp
The splendor of pure music
And the mystery of life.

*

To walk through the wall
Of death
How
Trance allows being toward Truth
To experience the unknown
As the reality
Of the close at hand
Dissolves into the always
Already there.

So
Eagle Hawk opens
His third eye
To the mystery of life
As being and nothingness
Trigger the authentic article
To dwell in the muscle and blood
Of what matters.

Then
Annabelle Lee trumpets
The moment
As the metaphor
Of The Unknown God
Defines another reality.

There is
The logic
Of another order
In this moment
And eternity awakens
Phenomenal reality
To the way, the Truth
And the life.

Then
The Unknown God
Takes being toward Truth
Into a house
Of many mansions
And the treasures
Of what matters
Fill the experiential
With the splendor
Of blessed assurance.

So
Annabelle Lee rides
The thunder of forevermore
While Eagle Hawk stands
Within the thought
That he finds in the beyond.

How
Meditation on The Word
Brings the mind
Into the vastness
Of possibility
As Truth pyramids
The heart into pure music.

*

Meditating on The Word
Annabelle Lee climbs
Into the other side
Of time and space
Where the splendor
Of pure music flourishes
And the trumpets
Of forevermore lead the way
Into the mystery of life.

There is
A portal of Truth
In the heart
Of being toward Truth
That takes the spirit
Far into the unknown.

Leaving the dull round
She collects moments
In a one-dimensional reality.

Then
Time and times
And a half erupted
With determination
As the children of promise
Marched into battle.

It was
A war of principalities
That consumed
The world
A war that hungered
For death.

To serve
The Unknown God
As patriots of freedom
How
Lady Liberty defended
The ramparts of Truth
And Annabelle Lee built
A fortress in mind.

It was
Victory in the hands
Of destiny
That the children
Of promise possessed
As they thundered
Across time and space.

Then
The sea parts
And eternity carries Truth
Into the heart of the earth.

Then
Mind dwells in the peace
Beyond understanding.

To feel
The victory of Truth
How
Meditation reveals
The mystery
Of the way, the Truth
And the life.

*

To connect to the beyond
Through meditation
Eagle Hawk focused
Upon his third eye
As he removed being toward Truth
From time and space.

It was
The energy of the deep touch
That drew him
Into a two-dimensional reality
Where thought pictured
The rise of a one-dimensional
Reality.

Then
The image
Of a golden calf
Melted in the moment
And the here and now
Turned into darkness.

A chill swept
Across his face
And shadows appeared
In his heart.

As the quick of life
Surrounded him
He felt his mind
Drift across the edge
Of being and nothingness.

Suddenly
A shaft of light
Struck him
Bringing him
Into the interstices
Of a looking glass.

He was
Both there and not there
At the same time.

Then
Vestiges of time past
Flashed
Across the horizon
And his third eye caught
A trace through the unknown.

There was
An inkling of hidden meaning
Written upon the walls
Of mind
As the way, the Truth
And the life disclosed
The mystery of life.

Then
The Unknown God
Formed him
Into the substance
Of being beyond self
That which is pure music.

*

As the children of promise
Witnessed the rise
Of fortresses in the sky
The moon eclipsed
Time and space
And Grandpa Time
Held the moment
In the palm of his mind.

Among the living
There was the taste
Of destiny
The acrid flavor
Of death to freedom.

It was
The picture of disaster
The crushing
Of Mother Earth
Beneath the heel
Of crazed despots
And terror flowed
With the blood
Of times and a half.

In the heart
Of each child of promise
Rose the courage
Of a patriot
And they headed out
To seize the day.

Lady Liberty led the charge
In the war of principalities
As the land of the free and brave
Struck down the power mongers
And the sun rose
Binging light
From the way, the Truth
And the life.

Then
Grandpa Time signaled
The victory of Truth
Over the puppet master's deceit
And he threw them
Into a pit of darkness.

Then
Pure music restored hope
To the world
As the land
Turned to peace
Beyond understanding
And The Unknown God
Blessed the earth.

How
The strongholds of freedom
Determined destiny.

How
The children of promise
Formed a more perfect union
To preserve and protect
Life, liberty
And the pursuit of happiness
For all.

*

To probe the mystery of life
Annabelle Lee
Connected to the deep touch
Through her third eye
Leaving phenomenal reality
For a parabola of time.

At first
There was the traffic
Of spurious thought
But as she plunged
Toward the center of the beyond
Pure music pictured
The substance of what matters.

Then
A portal to the other side
Of time and space
Appeared
As she took flight
Into the rhythm
Of the drums of eternity.

Passing
Through celestial dynasties
She felt the presence
Of The Unknown God
As possibility formed
The vision of Truth.

Time and space dissolved
In the waters of mind
As a message was written
Upon the wall of death.

Walking through that wall
She felt the breath
Of life fill her
With visions of forevermore.

Then
Her third eye penetrated
The source of hope
As The Word gave her
The peace beyond understanding.

It was
That a vision of eternity
Came through her faith
Carrying her on the wings
Of always and forever.

Then
The deep touch
Of The Unknown God
Gave her blessed assurance.

So
Through meditation
She grasped
The mystery of life.

*

Gathering in the garden
Of tables and chairs
The patriots
Readied for battle
As Lady Liberty rose
In their blood.

They were dressed
In the full armor
Of The Unknown God
Armed with determination.

They were ready
To fight the good fight.

Grandpa Time stood
Among them
Pointing to the way
The Truth and the life
As they mounted
Their ride to destiny.

Traveling through
The back roads
And alley ways
With hot lead
Defining the moment
The patriots owned
Into their mission
To defend
The land of the free and brave.

What once was
A land of milk and honey
Turned into a hot bed
Of revolt
As domestic terrorists
Crippled the country.

Annabelle Lee led the troops
Into conflict, as the sun set
And darkness drew out
The anarchists.

Cowering in the shadows
The terrorists hid
Waiting for a time to strike.

Revolt was not in the heart
Of the children of promise
The multitude of citizens
Who only wanted
To work and live
In peace
Providing for their family.

Revolt was a movement
Fueled by foreign concerns
And power mongers
Alien nations determined
To tear down freedom
And enslave the populace
Puppet masters who

Wanted to control
The hearts and minds
Of the children of promise.

*

On a star lit night
Annabelle Lee wanders
With the moon
Around the mountains
Of Tennessee.

Her footsteps echo
Across times and a half
As pure music
Follows her in the shadows.

Visiting his dreams
Of Eagle Hawk
She reaches into his heart
With a deep touch
And he feels
Her warm kiss carry him
Through a wilderness
Of splendor.

Embraced by the image
Of her silhouette
His bones ache
With passion
And eternity opens
The Book of Life.

How
Love sweats in the darkness.

Then
A song weaves
A pattern of forevermore
Into the fabric
Of being toward Truth
As Annabelle Lee
Undresses time and space.

There is
The form of another reality
One that lingers
On the tongue of mind
One that writes Truth
In start light.

How
The moon enlightens the trace
To the always already there
As visions picture
The peace beyond understanding.

So
The endless night
Of endless dreams
Brings an awakening
To the way
The Truth and the life.

Then
The Unknown God
Fills the moment
With blessed assurance
As Annabelle Lee rests
At the side of Eagle Hawk.

*

As Eagle Hawk distanced
Himself from the dull round
He looked through a portal
To the beyond
And his faith
In The Unknown God
Grew more and more solid.

In pursuit of Truth
He had wandered
Through the wilderness
Of thought
Finding no end
To possibility.

Across time and space
Eternity wrote the way
The Truth and the life
With the blood
Of the sacrificial lamb.

Reading through the lines
Eagle Hawk saw his iniquities
Blotted out
As the grace of The Word
Looked beyond his faults.

How
The trumpets of forevermore
Awakened the moment
To the peace beyond understanding
As his meditation defined
The always already there
And the celestial clocks
Pronounced destiny in his heart.

Then
He envisioned a land
Of milk and honey
Devoured by hate
With the children of promise
Cast into turmoil.

It was
A war of hearts and minds
That ripped life
Into shreds
Of bloody meat.

It was
A war of principalities
That plunged a dagger
Into the heart of Truth.

How
Eagle Hawk felt
A deep sadness at the thought
Of the death of the land
Of the free and brave.

*

As the sun awakens
The dawn of thought
The mind reflects
Upon the existential moment
Through meditation
And the third eye
Searches for Truth
Among the living and the dead.

Removing the mask
Of self-deception
Annabelle Lee shows her face
To destiny
As her mind travels
Into the far reaches
Of possibility.

Among the shadows
Of being and nothingness
Her meditation takes her
Far beyond the here and now
And there, her third eye
Gathers thoughts of Truth
From hidden meaning.

Since reading between the lines
Of life reveals the way
The Truth and the life
Annabelle Lee awakens
To the Truth
Of The Unknown God.

Then
The looking glass of forevermore
Takes her into the deep touch
And she feels the stir
Of pure music in her vitals.

How
Truth triumphs
Over a world of darkness
As the light of The Word
Allows being toward Truth
To feel the presence of freedom
As the heart pumps life
Into the living dead.

Then
Leaving the shadows
Of self deception
She envisions
The call onto forevermore
As she follows Truth
Into the everlasting.

So
The mind clears
As the pure heart dwells
In the peace
Beyond understanding.

So
Her faith carries her
Into a house of many mansions
After a while.

*

Searching
For the authentic article
In a wilderness of thought
Annabelle Lee configures
The substance of being toward Truth
Through the looking glass
Of forevermore
As the drums of eternity
Carry her heart
Into the always already there.

Bleeding the moment
Inside phenomenal reality
The very interstices
Of time and space
Her third eye perceives
The mystery of life
In the minute particular.

Then
Being toward Truth climbs
Into the other side
Of possibility
As a vision of Truth
Takes to pure music
And the presence
Of the deep touch molds
Being and nothingness
Into what is there.

Then
Annabelle Lee walks
Through the wall of death.

It is
That the authentic article
Dwells in the presence
Of The Unknown God
And enters the experiential
Through blessed assurance.

It is
That the authentic article
Emanates from Truth
The hidden meaning that resides
In pure music.

Then
Annabelle Lee reaches
Into the unknown
As a vertical column of time
Takes her
Into an existential awakening.

Then
Thought unearths nonbeing
And the third eye envisions
The way
The Truth and the life.

So
Truth becomes the blood
Of the authentic article.

So
The authentic article
Emerges
From cosmic consciousness
Through a wilderness
Of thought.

Then
Her mind clears
As the given pumps life
Back into her pure heart.

*

Taken by the morning star
As the dawn awakened
The here and now
Lady Liberty advanced
Through the unknown
To drink in the pure music
Of the always already there.

Her third eye welcomed
The way, the Truth and the life
With a thirst
Aching in her dry bones.

Then free spirits
Brought the deep touch
From The Unknown God
Into her vision
As cosmic consciousness
Infused the calling
Onto forevermore.

She saw the children
Of promise
Led into darkness
As their minds yielded
To clever rhetoric.

The world had taught
That slavery provided them
With all their wants and needs
And they submitted
To the treachery
Of the puppet masters.

There was, however
A pocket of patriots
A remnant of Truth
That lived with The Word
In their heart.

They carried the message of Truth.

They rose with the sun
And followed pure music
Through the unknown
As the trumpets of destiny
Pyramided Truth
Into the here and now.

They were not slaves to the puppet masters.

They chose to serve The Unknown God.

Then, Lady Liberty led the charge to freedom.

*

So
The puppet masters hide
Behind their clever rhetoric
Inciting fear across a land
Of milk, and honey
As they hunger for power.

Turning against the will
Of the people, they
Flaunt their talking points
As if their words were true
When all they want
Is to strengthen the muscle
Of power mongers.

They grip the throat of freedom
Strangling the hopes
And dreams of a nation.

They speak of healing a nation
As they gouge out
The heart of the people.

So
The life of the free and brave
Faces destiny
As children starve
Because of a lack of Truth.

So
A generation is taught
That it is entitled
Which is true
But it is entitled
To the good and the bad
According to their own making.

To be a slave
To their own ignorance
How very, very sad.

To have only
The god of their stomach
Believing in the right
Of their own wants and needs
How very, very sad
To think they are privileged.

Soon
The trumpet will sound
And the di, it will be cast.

To put their trust
In puppet masters
How they may prove
To be the victims
Of their own folly.

Then
Their destiny will live
In a shallow grave.

*

In a valley of promise
An old man stumbles
Toward his destiny
The wisdom of the ages
Upon his tongue.

Following the flight
Of the crows
He leaves traces
In the wind
As his mind focuses
Upon being and nothingness.

In his blood Truth prospers
As a given
Because he has witnessed
The work
Of The Unknown God.

How
Hungry the heart that hears
Pure music in time
And times and a half
As the calling
From the always already there
Liberates his mind onto seeing clearly
The way, the Truth and the life.

So
He believes himself
Into being toward Truth
A presence, unearthed
From the existential moment
And the face that he wears
Beams with hope
Because his years
Have taught him well.

Then
He enters a wilderness
Of thought
As trumpets sound
Announcing the birth
Of forevermore
And he stands
Before the awakening
Of another reality

The old man, then
Walks through the wall
Of death
As promise fills
His heart with life.

To be the very presence
Of pure music
Becomes his destiny.

*

In a valley of promise
An old man stumbles
Toward his destiny
The wisdom of the ages
Upon his tongue.

Following the flight
Of crows
He leaves traces
In the wind
To the mystery of life
As his mind focuses
Upon being and nothingness.

In his blood Truth prospers
As a given
Because he has
witnessed the work
Of The Unknown God.

How
Hungry the heart
That hears the pure music
In time and times
And a half
As the calling
Of the always already there
Liberates his mind
Until he sees clearly
The way to Truth
And the life.

So
He believes himself
Into being toward Truth
A presence unearthed
From the existential moment
And the face
That he wears
Beams with hope
Because his years
Have taught him well.

Then
He enters a wilderness
Of thought
And trumpets sound
Announcing the birth
Of forevermore
As he stands
Before eternity
An awakening to Truth.

The old man
Then
Walks through the wall
Of death
A promise filling
His heart with life.

To be the presence
Of pure music
Becomes his destiny.

*

Through a looking glass
Clouds form a shroud
Around the way to Truth
As the mind wrestles
with the mystery of life.

Awakening to the moment
When the dawn of thought
Traces meaning through footsteps
In time and space
Annabelle Lee listens
To pure music driven
Through the reflection
Of a two-dimensional reality.

According to the celestial clocks
The unknown bleeds
Into the image of time
And times and a half
As she feels the deep touch
Lift her mind
Onto a portal to the beyond.

It is not magic
That presents the thought
Of traveling
Into the center of what matters
But it is pure music
That delivers her
Through the wilds
Of being and nothingness.

As the clouds disappear
The vision that is there
In the looking glass
Becomes the way, the Truth
And the life
And reflections of hope
Form destiny.

Then
Pure music liberates her
From the bondage
To the dull round
As the moment
Passes into forevermore.

Then
A vertical column of time
Unfolds layers of the actual
And Annabelle Lee reaches
The peace beyond understanding.

She feels the deep touch
Reaching into her heart
Carrying her with the rhythm
Of the drums of eternity.

Then
Cosmic consciousness
Kisses her
With the mystery of life.

So
Phenomenal reality
Is the form of the actual
The very substance
Of what is.

*

Unearthing time and space
In search of Truth
She connected
To cosmic consciousness
Through meditation
As she passed
Through the looking glass
Of being and nothingness.

It was
The surfacing
Of being toward Truth
Beyond the here and now
That brought mind
To the threshold
Of nonbeing.

As the drums of eternity
Pounded the rhythm
Of pure music
Into the moment
She took to a two
Dimensional reality
And thought exploded
The domain
Of linear time and space.

Then
Annabelle Lee pulled
The substance
Of hidden meaning
From the dull round.

There was
The rise of the living moment
From the mystery of life
And Annabelle Lee followed
The way
The Truth and the life.
Into forevermore.

Then
Nonbeing took her
To the peace
Beyond understanding
Infused with the ultimate power
Of The Unknown God.

As her trance
Embodied the deep touch
She read the splendor
Of a vertical column of time
And The Spirit of Wisdom
Allowed her entrance
Into a one-dimensional reality.

Then
With the presence
Of pure music in her heart
She felt Truth
From the always already there.

*

Dragging himself
Through futility
He feels darkness
As despair takes him
Beneath time and space
And his heart withers
his dry bones rattle.

All life left him
With no reason
To carry on
And nothingness sinks
The moment.

With a twelve-pack
Before him
And a carving knife
In his right hand
He decides when
He finishes the last
Can of beer
He will fall on the blade.

Disgusted with his life
Disgusted with the world
He finds no reason
To continue this cruel joke
Called life
As he drinks himself
Into a void.

Dread surrounds him.

Looking into a mirror
He sees the face of death
The meaninglessness
That has captured his life.

He looks
Into the work
Of his hands
Seeing the callousness
Of his heart.

How
Much of his vision
Was blinded
By being of the world.

Curious as it is
He fell into a drunken stupor
Before he used the knife.

Curious as it is
When he woke up
He carried on.

After a while
He found the way
To cultivate the earth
Of his life
Allowing his own seed
To prosper and grow
In the knowledge
Of The Unknown God.

So
He was set aside
To witness the work
Of the way
The Truth and the life.

*

SECTION 3:
The dance of forevermore

It is
That it was a moment
To venture
Into the unknown
To unearth
The mystery of life
Because the shadows
Cast by the dull round
Hid the way to the actual.

Reflecting in the mirror
Of what was there
Eagle Hawk took
To a two-dimensional reality
As he studied the elements
Of phenomenal reality.

A message was written
Between the lines of stars
And planets and swirling orbs
Signaling the image
Of things in themselves
To don a mask
Of nothingness.

Seeing through a forest
Of possibility
Where light reached
The mind
He deciphered
The deep touch
Through a parabola
Of time.

As he rode the rhythm
Of the drums of eternity
Into a portal to the beyond
The moment moved
His heart into the language
Of the always already there.

His tranced allowed him
To advance
Into the other side
Of time and space
The dwelling place
Of the unknown.

Eagle Hawk felt the rise
Of nonbeing
Into the spirit
Of being toward Truth
And a vertical column
Of time crushed darkness
And the shadows
Of darkness.

Then
With light behind
His third eye
He dug into the earth
Of the mystery of life
Finding the actual
As the presence
Of The Unknown God.

Then
Eagle Hawk became pure music
Embraced by the peace
Beyond understanding
And the power of forevermore.

*

To feel the pure music
In being toward Truth
She reached
Into the substance
Of the close at hand
Through trancing
And z parabola of time
Took her
To the other side
Of time and space.

As she walked
Through a valley
Of dry bones
The shadows cast
By a starry night
Encompassed the moment
And the moon moved
Her mind
Behind the mask
of being and nothingness.

Then
The world danced
To the rhythm
Of the drums of eternity.

Then
A song carried her
Behind the crumbling walls
Of self-deception
As an intruder marked
Time and times and a half
As the beginning
Of a new age.

Trumpets sounded.

Flags of freedom worked
Their way into the sky.

It is
That it was
A moment in thee heat
Of five hours that p0ierced
The side of what matters
And the dull round cheered.

What grief.

Sad to witness
The brutalization
Of the way
The Truth and the life.

Then
A har rain flooded
All and everything
With no sight of land
For forty days and forty nights.

Then
She felt the deep touch
Of pure music
Take her into the presence
Of The Unknown God.

*

The purple mountains
Rising in their majesty
Witness pure music
Pyramiding
Through the heart and mind
Of Lady Liberty.

She has come
To a people
That honors freedom
As they write
Upon the tablets
Of destiny.

Their message spills
Upon a world
That knows bondage.

The blood of Truth
Rejoices in her presence.

So
Patriots march to the anthem
Of stars and stripes
As Lady Liberty stands
For the human rights
For every man, every woman
And every child.

In a world that hungers
For peace
She brings the bread and wine
Of life, liberty
And the pursuit of happiness.

She is a beacon of light
Guiding a world into the dawn
Of an age when all life matters.

She holds Truth in one hand
And justice in the other
As she serves the world
With honor and dignity.

Her beauty and strength
Carry the age
Into the victory
Of freedom over oppression.

Although all nations
Know fault in their past
Her future offers them
A more perfect union
Founded upon the grace
Of God.

So
Lady Liberty sings
With pure music
In her heart and mind
From every valley
And mountain top
Across every land.

*

A mystery tree bleeds
On a hill called Golgotha
As a life of Truth hangs
A testament
To The Unknown God.

Weaving through the air
The smell of death
Fills the moment
Asa agony pronounces
The fullness of time.

Darkness descends
Upon the earth
As thunder penetrates
The witnesses
And their hopes
Weep over the death
Of Truth.

Ravaged by the times
The beath of hope
Joins the no longer
As a people know
Not what they do.

Laid in a tomb
A body rests still but on the third day
Life is restored
And Truth walks onto the always
Already there
Restoring hope in the witnesses
To the way, the Truth and the life.

It is
The dawn of a new age
That conquers fear
And comforts the weary.

Certainly
Death has no dominion.

So
The blind see, the deaf hear
And the crippled dance
As the only begotten Son
Of The Unknown God
Shepherds a flock
Onto a house
Of many mansions
Onto the peace
Beyond understanding.

Then
The trumpets sound
Because Truth, victorious
Lives forevermore.

*

Listening to the rhythm
Of the heart of eternity
He engaged his mind
To pursue Truth
As pure music took him
Into a space beyond time
And he knelt before a river
Seeing the reflection
Of the always already there.

Then
The mystery of life
Covered his eyes
With clouds of being
And nothingness
As the world gasped
With a last breath.

Since his desire was to know Truth
His mind focused on nonbeing
As his trance rose
Through hidden meaning.

Then
The substance
Of phenomenal reality
Lifted him
Out of the waters
Of possibility
And The Unknown God
Gave him The Word
Revealing hidden meaning.

As the heart of eternity
Pumped an elixir
Of power and strength
Into his substance
His thought carried him
Into the everlasting
And trust filed him
With a vision
Of what matters.

As the clouds
Of being and nothingness
Disappeared
His inner being looked
Through his third eye
And understanding
Colored his vision
With the way to Truth and life.

As he walked with The Word
He felt the call to witness
End times
And cosmic consciousness
Filled his world with the vision
To serve pure music
The will of The Unknown God.

*

Rising into the sky
Where nonbeing presents
Power and grace
Annabelle Lee ventures
Into the unknown
Reading the signs
That lead to understanding.

She navigates
Across endless possibility
With her mind quickened
By the drums of eternity
Although the call
Of a crow touches her
With the here and now.

Torn between her want
To grasp hidden meaning
And the grip of the mask
Of self-deception
She takes
To a parabola of time
As the moment stills.

Then
The physics
Of the other side
Of time and space
Awaken thought
To the way
The Truth and the life.

Then
The feel of being toward Truth
Registers pure music
And the voice
Of the everlasting
Stirs the heart
Into the living moment.

Seeing the grandeur
Of The Unknown God
Annabelle Lee surfaces
Through a looking glass
Onto time and times
And a half.

There is
Truth behind the wall
Of the here and now
That allows hidden meaning
To appear as images
In nonbeing.

So
Nonbeing overflows
With the deep touch
As Annabelle Lee witnesses
The mystery
Of a vertical column of time.

Then
She knows the life of Truth
In forevermore.

*

To know Truth
An old man climbed
Out of himself
As his mind carried
Being toward Truth into orbits
Of possibility.

He was charged
With the gravity
Of being and nothingness
As he walked
Through one reality
After another
Following the rhythm
Of pure music.

Arriving at the edge
Of end times
He mounted the wings
Of forevermore
And flew
Through the mirror
Of the always already there.

Then
He became echoes
Of his times
As cosmic consciousness
Inhaled his substance.

A southern breeze
Took the old man
To the other side
Of being and time
And what was there
Wrote his substance
Into the Book of Life.

It was
A moment when his trance
Revealed untapped layers
Of mind.

Then
The deep touch reached
Into his heart
Restoring the breath of his life
And he stepped back
Into what he knew as himself.

Returning
To the here and now
He felt pure music
Integrate his moment
With Truth.

So
The form and substance
Of being toward Truth exists
To follow the way
The Truth and the life.

So
The Spirit of Wisdom
Smiles upon the old man.

*

Taking to a channel
To the beyond
Annabelle Lee pyramided
The way
The Truth and the life
As her meditation
Encompassed forevermore.

As a burst of stars
Opened the moment
To the other side
Of time and space
She pictured pure music
Dancing through the wilds
Of mind
And thought trumpeted
The unknown
Into being toward Truth.

Then
The drums of eternity
Delivered the peace
Beyond understanding
And the power
Of the always already there.

It was
An adventure
Into the mystery of life
As she climbed
Out of self
As she rode the rhythm
Of a parabola of time
As she eclipsed
The existential moment
Of being and nothingness.

Then
She walked through the wall
That surrounds
A house of many mansions
Finding her place
In time and times
And a half.

Connecting to the source
Of all and everything
She felt the deep touch
Of The Unknown God
Allowing her life
Liberty and the pursuit
Of happiness.

Returning to the here
And now
From her trance
She knew her birth
As a child of promise
Because she saw
Her name written
In The Book of Life.

So
She carried on with her love
From the Spirit of Wisdom.

*

Feeling the deep touch
Of The Unknown God
She channeled the way
The Truth and the life
As her third eye
Opened her vision
To The Spirit of Wisdom.

Then
Cosmic consciousness
Pumped life into her heart
As the morning dawned
Out of darkness.

So
Lady Liberty faced
The moment
With courage and clarity
Prepared for battle
Against the power mongers
And domestic terrorists.

To witness and defend
Truth
Was her mission
As she led
The children of promise
In the war
Of principalities.

So
Annabelle Lee and the patriots
Geared up
Locked and loaded
As they secured the perimeter
As the star spangle banner
Waved freedom across the land
Of milk and honey.

They would not
Lay down their arms
And would not submit
To the cancel culture.

They would
Fight for freedom
From sea to shining sea.

Armed to the teeth
She held her ground
Ready to face the destiny
Of the free world.

So
Time moved quickly
Toward the flash point.

So
It was peace through strength.

*

Looking through a window
Where all and everything rots
They drink in despair
As the language of nothingness
Writes desolation
Into the moment.

It is
A time within
The here and now
That takes the world
Into the gauntlet of the war
Of principalities.

Then
The dirge
Of out living self
Tears their heart apart
As their bones
Crumble beneath the weight
Of times and a half.

There is no
Light in their ye
As darkness chokes
Their vision
As the cold freezes
Their mind
And their thoughts
Die in isolation.

They have forgotten
The way
The Truth and the life.

They have left their meditation
Upon The Word for the babble
Of the dull round.

Although
They turned away
From The Unknown God
The Spirit of Wisdom
Speaks to their heart
Calling them
Onto the way, the Truth
And the life.

So
Their freewill determines
Their destiny.

*

An old man stood
Before the dawn
Of forevermore
As the world spun
Wildly out of control
And his meditation
Reached into time
And times and a half.

Among the workings
Of the celestial clocks
He envisioned a battlefield
In a valley of dry bones
During the war of principalities.

Sitting beneath
A banyan tree
He meditated upon the way
The Truth and the life.

A river of blood
In a valley of dry bones.
Took his thought
Onto the destiny
Of the dull round.

It was
The hunger of power mongers
That he could not understand.

How
They manipulated language
Into half-truths
At the expense of freedom.

How
Their clever minds
Spelled deception
With pride
As they dug
An unmarked grave
For Lady Liberty.

So
The old man heard
The weeping of the world
As he yearned
For the return of freedom.

As his trance ended
And he returned
To the here and now
The old man saw the sadness
Of the sunset.

*

Submerged in the language
Of the always already there
They connect to the way
The Truth and the life
As a harvest moon
Pyramids forevermore
Into the moment.

Among the backroads
Of mind
They find the mystery
Of life
Basking in starlight
As pure music carries them
Into the substance
Of what matters.

Then
They hear the trumpets
Of forevermore
Pronounce the birth
Of a new age
And the world trembles
Before the thought
Of the deep touch.

So
The children of promise
Embraced the reckoning
In time and times and a half.

Then
They faced the war
Of principalities
With the courage
Given to them
By The Unknown God
And they won hearts
To Truth
As the harvest moon
Witnessed their call to faith.

It was
The victory of life
Over death that brought
The children of promise
Into the house
Of many mansions

As pure music conquered
The noise of the world.

How
Staying in The Word
Brought strength
To the children of promise
As they sought a clear mind
And a pure heart.

So
The language of Truth
Liberated an age
From self-deception.

*

Across the dawn of time and space
Mind travels through meditation
Into pure music, as the deep touch
Reaches into being toward Truth.

As a vision of the house
Of many mansions
Fills the moment
Splendor radiates
From a vertical column of time
And she walks onto the unknown
Ever so cautiously.

Then
Her third eye opens
A two-dimensional reality
As the moon dresses in darkness
And Annabelle Lee paints
The mystery of life
With the sweat of love.

As memories dance
In the body
Of pure music
The wind carries
Her song
Onto the deep touch
And Lady Liberty
Waves the flag
Of stars and stripes.

How
Mind pictures the trace
To the beyond
As freedom celebrates
Th life of Truth.

How
Being and nothingness
Shatter dreams of pure music
As a patriot returns
To the here and now
With thoughts
Of Annabelle Lee.

Then
He bleeds into the sand
Of a distant land
His memory lost
In time and space.

*

The crows have come
To deliver a message
From the beginning
Of times and a half
That moment
Of veritable reality
When hidden meaning
Dressed the way
The Truth and the life
With glory.

It is
A fullness of time
That moves the mind
To celebrate the gift
Of light to those
Living in darkness
As the crows liberate
The children of promise
With hope.

It is
The gathering of dreams
Fed by the dance
Of the crows in the sky
That awakens being toward Truth
To pure music.

Then
Visions of the deep touch
Allow eternity to dwell
In the here and now.

Then
The crows open the door
To the peace
Beyond understanding
Through the work
Of The Word
And the children of promise
Rejoice.

How
The living moment
Restores the presence of Truth
Through the power
Of The Unknown God.

How
Cosmic consciousness
Pictures what is there
As the victory
Over oppression
As the puppet masters
Fall into oblivion.

It is
The demise
Of the power mongers
By their own folly
That the crows pronounce
In their message.

So
The crows speak Truth
Into the moment
Forevermore.

*

Although the old man
Felt his age
In arthritic bones
He had the vision of eternity
In his heart
As he stepped
Into the unknown
And his mind colored
Phenomenal reality
With pure music.

It was
The workings
Of cosmic consciousness
That took him
Beyond time and space.

It was
The rhythm of the drums
Of eternity
That carried Truth
In his look
As a two-dimensional reality
Reflected the deep touch
In his third eye.

How
Walking in a parabola
Of time took him
To The Spirit of Wisdom
As his thoughts
Deconstructed time present.

Then
The old man
Connected to a channel
That led to the substance
Of being and nothingness
And the image of forevermore
Danced to the optics
Of pure music.

So
He left the ground
Of outliving self
As his want reached
The way
The Truth and the life.

So
He held what matters
In his mind
As The Unknown God
Allowed him the breath
Of being toward Truth.

Then
His heart orchestrated
Times and a half
Into a moment
That pyramided Truth
From the mystery of life
Into pure music.

*

Moving into the unknown
Undressing being and nothingness
She opened her third eye
To a parabola of time
Until The Spirit of Wisdom
Gave her a clear mind
And a pure heart
Through a portal
To a one-dimensional
Reality.

Then
Time and times and a half
Wrote the way
The Truth and the life
Upon being toward Truth.

Then
Her thoughts consumed
The mystery of life
As she hungered
For the moment of pure music.

As her trance took her
Far beyond time and space
The dawn of what matters
Awakened her to the peace
Beyond understanding
And the power
Of The Unknown God
Filled her
With cosmic consciousness.

Then
She heard the drums
Of eternity.

So
The moment cleansed her
Of self-deception.

It was
The launching
Of an epiphany
That brought pure music
Into her heart
As her mind formed
A more perfect union
Between being and nothingness.

It was
The end of the war
Of principalities.

When she returned
To the here and now
The Spirit of Wisdom
Guided her with the language
Of the deep touch
Onto forevermore.

So
There is Truth
In being toward Truth.

*

As the artist configures
Pure music
With the color of dreams
The unknown pictures
The mystery of life
In the blood
Of being toward Truth.

There is
The articulation
Of being and nothingness
Through the deep touch
That liberates
Time and space
From the dull round
As the artist
Portrays the substance
Of what is there.

Traveling through mind
Where ideas are born
He births the life
Of agony and ecstasy
As an image of want
Hungers for Truth.

Then
Times and a half
Reach into the heart
With power and majesty
Guided by
The Spirit of Wisdom.

It is
The freedom of thought
Dancing upon the mindscape
That pyramids an image
From the always already there
Onto the presence of the way
The Truth and the life.

Then
Pure music infuses
The moment with echoes
Of Truth
Onto forevermore
And the heart follows
The rhythm of the drums
Of eternity.

Then
Being and nothingness
Portray
The figure and ground
Of the mystery of life
And the artist
Steps away

From the moment.

At the climax
Of time and space
The Unknown God
Smiles.

SECTION 4:
Toward substance

As pure music pyramids
The mystery of life
Into the substance of mind
The witness climbs
Into a two-dimensional reality
And The Spirit of Wisdom
Speaks life
Into being toward Truth.

There is
A chasm of darkness
Between thought
And what is there
As being and nothingness
Traces the journey
Beyond phenomenal reality
With the blood of what matters.

Then
Pure music becomes
The instrument of forevermore.

Then
The witness leaps through a portal
To a one-dimensional reality.

How
Trusting the way
The Truth and the life
Signals a starry night
Into dreams
And thought of dreams.

Following celestial clocks
Beyond time
The witness holds life
With a pocket of miracles
Sprinkling Truth
From the heavenly bodies
And folding hidden meaning
Into the pages of what matters.

So
There is a passageway
Through the darkness
Of the dull round
That leads to the gift
Of hope
And life returns
To the dry bones
Of the here and now.

Then
Pure music trumpets
The mystery of life
Into the witness
And The Unknown God
Speaks the authentic article
Into the children of promise.

So
The witness reads Truth
From The Book of Life.

*

While meditating
Seeing the grip
Of pure music
How
The heart beats
The deep touch
Into the moment
As the third eye searches
For the way to Truth and life.

Echoes of cosmic
Consciousness cascade
Through the universe
As the light
Of the fullness of time
throbs the muscle
Of what matters.

So
Pure music carries
The witness
Into visions of the celestial clocks
And trumpets sound
The beginning of the other side
Of phenomenal reality.

Leaving the dull round
And the tyranny
Of its madness
The witness unearths
Hidden meaning
From the graveyard
Of being and nothingness.

Then
the drums of bone and flesh
sweat life
into times and a half
as the trance
reveals a portal
to a one-dimensional
reality
and The Unknown God
allows beauty and wonder
to color the moment.

As the witness
Beholds the workings
Of The Spirit of Wisdom
Pure music encompasses
Being and nothingness
And the hope of a generation
Tells being toward Truth
The way, the Truth and the life
In the language
Of the always already there.

Then
Pure music forms
A more perfect symmetry
With life, liberty
And the pursuit of happiness.

*

With the language
Of The Spirit of Wisdom
The witness deciphered
The code of hidden meaning
As the mystery of life
Surfaced in the looking glass
And time present vanished
In the shadows
Of being and nothingness.

As pure music liberated
The dull round from bondage
A trace of Truth sang freedom
Onto the horizon of times and a half.

Then
The witness secured
The message of hope
In the dawn of thought.

Then
The third eye
Of being toward Truth grasped
The tongue
Of the puppet masters
As they choked on their words
And the language of Truth
Buried them
In an unmarked grave.

It was
The will of The Unknown God
That brought freedom
To the children of promise.

It was
The way, The Truth
And the life that rose
Through the looking glass.

So
The witness spoke freedom
Across a wasteland
As it turned into the land
Of mild and honey.

Guided by The Spirit of Wisdom
The witness shared pure music
As the children of promise
Dwelled with the mystery of life
In their heart.

So
The hidden meaning
That the power mongers conjured
No longer corrupted
Time and times and a half.

*

In the blaze of autumn
When the moon, full and bright
Shone through a starry night
Annabelle Lee heard
The trumpet of the always
Already there
As she stepped
Through a passageway
To cosmic consciousness.

As her trance took her
Far beyond the here and now
She witnessed Lady Liberty
Facing a firing squad
As the world spun
Out of control.

A river of blood
Carried the freedom
Of a generation
Into the abyss.

It was
A tragic vision
That tormented her.

Then
Annabelle Lee dressed
In the full armor
Of The Unknown God.

Then
She joined
The underground patriots.

It was
A war of principalities
That determined
The life of liberty.

Pulling out
Of her meditation
Annabelle Lee followed
The shadow of Lady Liberty
With the children of promise
In the march of freedom.

It was
An army of seventy million
Led by the muscle and blood
Of Lady Liberty
That demonstrated
Before the world
And the puppet masters
Trembled.

So
Time and times
And a half passed
As freedom returned
To the stars and stripes.

*

At the grave of Truth
The children of promise weep
And the ashes of freedom
Leave no trace.

How
Puppet masters twist
The language
Into daggers of deceit
As a people are led
To slaughter.

So
The powermongers lynch
Lady Liberty
And they cancel history
As they eliminate hope.

They crush the dreams
Of a people
As they erased the way
The Truth and the life.

So
The children of promise
Are crucified
Because of their faith
In The Unknown God.

Then
The days of darkness
Smother life
As the powermongers corrupt
The thoughts of the living.

So
The land of milk and honey
Turns into a vast wasteland.

There is
No future
But only the encompassing
Of despair in time present.

So
The beast has come
To devour Truth
And the world
Staggers into captivity.

Among the mountains
And deep in the forest
A remnant prepares
To liberate
A people from bondage
To restore hope
And to bring back
The freedom of Truth.

*

At the dawn of thought
Mind awakens
To endless possibility
And The Spirit of Wisdom_
Guides being toward Truth
Onto pure music;
However
There is the shadow of being
And nothingness in the heart
As the dull round grinds
Life into dust.

Across the horizon
Mind bleeds want of Truth
Into the moment
As time and space
Slip into the no longer.

It is
The death of freedom
That cancels Truth.

It is
The birth of tyranny
That murders hope.

Even in death
The life of liberty
Lives on.

Then
The heart engages the way
The Truth and the life
As The Spirit of Wisdom
Equips being toward Truth
With the power
Of The Unknown God.

Since
Destiny always sides
With Truth
The mind speaks
Inalienable rights
Across the landscape
And the children of promise
Believe themselves onto a clear mind
And a pure heart.

So
The powermongers
Void themselves
With their own folly
Because they are deaf
To pure music.

So
The puppet masters
Dangle from their own strings.

So
Lady Liberty triumphs
Over tyranny.

*

Listening to tunes
From long ago
She filled the room
With the light from her eyes
As being and nothingness
Collided with what matters.

There was
Blood on the wall
And a half living body
Crouched over wicker chair.

Looking out a window
She saw a man
Hanging from a white oak tree
And crows gathered
As the trumpets
Of the ever lasting
Echoed throughout
Her mind.

Pulling out of trance
She witnessed Lady Liberty
Triumphant over the puppet masters
And time present returned
From the other side
Of the sky
As tunes carried on.

Placing daisies in a crystal vase
She counted the patriots
Fallen in battle
And clouds of the always
Already there wept
Over lost hopes and dreams.

Then
She dressed possibility
With the way
The Truth and the life.

Then
She believed herself
Into being toward Truth
And The Spirit of Wisdom
Took her into pure music.

It was
A song that carried her
Through a looking glass
Onto a mercy seat.

It was
The rhythm of the drums
Of eternity
That brought her
Into the house
Of many mansions
Where she sang in the presence
Of The Unknown God.

*

As her trance
Took her to the heart
Of phenomenal reality
She rose into the unknown
Through a parabola of time
Where the celestial clocks
Defined being and nothingness.

It was
Being toward Truth
That fashioned the moment
As she felt the deep touch
Of cosmic consciousness
And her passion for life
Took her mind into pure music.

Crossing the expanse
Thoughts connected her heart
To the rhythm of eternity
As the look
Of what matters
Pointed to the way
The Truth and the life.

Then
The brilliance of a one
Dimensional reality
Dawned the mystery of life
In her mind
And dreams took her
Into the land
Of hidden meaning.

Dwelling there
Were the lives of Truth
And they opened her being
To the blood and bones
Of forevermore.

Then
The Spirit of Wisdom
Anointed her
As one of the children
Of promise
And her name was written
In The Book of Life.

Leaving the moment
She returned
To time and space
Carrying the message
Of her destiny.

Then
She danced in the presence
Of Truth
In the splendor
Of The Unknown God.

*

With the birth of ideation
The third eye paints
A horizon of times
And a half
As the physics of mind
Pyramids thoughts of the way
The Truth and the life.

Traveling beyond
The here and now
She collects fragments
Of hidden meaning
And she places them
In her heart.

How
The blood of what matters
Carries her
Onto the mystery of life
And the moment points
To The Unknown God.

Then
She walks through the graves
Of time past
As Truth echoes endless possibility
Into a full measure of dreams.

Connecting
To the inner reaches
Of time and space
She follows a portal
To cosmic consciousness
As her heart bleeds
The want of Truth.

Then
She understands
That Truth is not a thing in itself
But is to be lived
And that her dance is a message
That defines Truth.

So
To be true
To have a clear mind
And a pure heart
Allows her to accept
The treasures
Of The Spirit of Wisdom.

To be called
To faith as one
Of the children of promise
Is sufficient-in-itself.

Then
She sees two old men
One black and one white
Walk over a hill together.

So
Truth dissolves confusion.

*

Through a looking glass
The mystery of life reached
From the unknown
Into being toward Truth
As she meditated
Upon the way
The Truth and the life.

It was
A moment in a vertical
Column of time
That brought the peace
Beyond understanding
Into her heart
As she drank in
The abundance of pure music
Flowing from the deep touch.

Suddenly
Being toward Truth
Unmasked hidden meaning
And the unknown
Filled her with endless
Possibility.

She was there and not there
At the same time.

She was filled
With pure music
As being toward Truth
Grounded her substance
In the always already there.

Then
The Spirit of Wisdom
Awakened her mind
To the glory
Of The Unknown God.

So
She understood Truth
Is not a thing in itself
But is to be lived
As her dance
Through time and space.

Then
As being toward Truth
She traveled through possibility
Harvesting the physics
Of pure music.

So
Her name as Lady Liberty
Was written into The Book
Of Life.

*

Walking through the unknown
As the mystery of life
Wrote the way
The Truth and the life
Upon her heart
She heard pure music
Echo across the expanse.

There was
An opening to the substance
Of bring and nothingness
As she hungered for Truth.

Then
The drums of eternity
Led the march
Of the children of promise
Onto the mountains
Of forevermore
As she witnessed
The play of the other side
Of time and space.

Feeling the deep touch
Of The Spirit of Wisdom
She wept
Because the moment
Shadowed pure music
As being toward Truth
Rubbed life into the dying.

There was
The dangling of possibility
From the mystery tree
As she climbed out of herself
And time present
Disappeared from the window
Of the actual.

Then
Hidden meaning carved
The mystery of life
Into what was there
As her trance carried her
Far beyond thought.

Then
She unearthed the unknown.

The
The mystery of life
Defined itself
Through pure music.

Sitting upon the mercy seat
She felt the love
Of The Unknown God
Cleanse her and she was healed.

So
She learned to follow
The way, the Truth and the life
From there on.

*

Dancing across rapids of fear
On the wings of pure music
She followed treasures born
Through being toward Truth
And she gathered waves
Of life from eternity.

There was
A song in her heart
That formed touch stones
To the way
The Truth and the life.

As the rhythm of the moment
Released her from the jaws
Of being and nothingness
She fed her tears
To wilderness rivers
As she looked into the eyes
Of the always already there.

So
She danced in the looking glass
Of times and a half.

So
She found herself
As being toward Truth.

Then
The Spirit of Wisdom kissed
Her mind.

Then
A vision of the peace
Beyond understanding
Took her into the love
Of The Unknown God.

It was
The light of pure music
That orchestrated
The deep touch
As her dance
Unchained possibility.

As she undressed reality
Hidden meaning rose
From wilderness rivers
And she unearthed
The dreams
Of the children of promise.

So
The mystery of life
Surfaces through her dance.

*

Down by the river
With visions of Grandpa Time
Sitting beneath a banyan tree
She recalled her voyage
Into the unknown
Where Truth etched the destiny
Of the children of promise.

From the encompassing
Pure music gathered
In her heart
As the vital signs
Of being toward Truth
Followed a trace
To the always already there.

While Grandpa Time fed
Sparrows breadcrumbs
Her third eye pyramided
A wilderness of thought
Onto her mind
As her trance connected her
To waves of possibility.

There was
A message there
From hidden meaning.

There was
A river of blood
From the everlasting.

There was
Life between the sparrows
And the children of promise.

How
The gravity
Of being and nothingness
Sunk her mind into the abyss
While her trance sought
The treasures
Of The Spirit of Wisdom.

To be stabbed
By the blade of memories
To be buried
In the grave of silence
She ended her voyage.

Then
Grandpa Time walked
Into her mind
With The Book of Life.

SECTION 5:
The rhythm of the everlasting

It was
An overture in blue
That brought being toward Truth
On to a moment
With the authentic article
As the mask of being there
Drifted away.

So
Grandpa Time pulled
Cosmic consciousness
Into the moment.

Then
He unearthed hidden meaning
From graves
Of endless possibility
Releasing pure music
Into a celebration
Of a one-dimensional reality.

As the geography of mind
Rose from the blue sea
Thoughts floated
In the deep touch
And time present sunk
Into the abyss.

So
Grandpa Time looked
Into the center
Of time and space
Finding the way
The Truth and the life.

Then
He colored the actual
With an overture in blue
Liberating being toward Truth
From the dull round.

As the drums of eternity
Awakened existential thought
Grandpa Time read
From The Book of Life
Allowing his presence
To feel The Spirit of Wisdom.

Then
He sat upon the mercy seat
In the garden
Of tables and chairs
Witnessing the workings
Of The Unknown God.

So
The celestial clocks
Chimed the hour
When Grandpa Time
Fulfilled his destiny.

*

Standing before the edge
Of the abyss
When the moment
Drowned in the blood
Of the time past
The artist articulates
The substance
Of s solitary wicker chair
As the heart yearns
For Truth.

It is
Th vision
Of hidden meaning
The desolation
Of the lost that emerges
On the canvas
As shadows form
The destiny of life.

Then
the colors
of pure music stir
the always already there
into the existential moment
as the witness
of life emerges
from death.

Seeking deliverance
From torment
The artist
Struggles with thoughts
As the mind dwells in absence
And the wicker chair
Empties life of its tears.

So
The witness connects
The image
To being and nothingness
As despair flows
Through a parabola of time
And being toward Truth
Finds life
At the edge of the abyss.

So
The wicker chair
Offers deliverance
As the emblem
Of the mercy seat
And the artist reaches
Through nothingness
With the deep touch.

Living in a moment
Of time past
The witness feels
The hidden meaning
In the mystery of life
As the presence
Of the artist lives on.

*

Running wild
Through the back roads
Of mind
She escaped
From the dull round
And headed toward
The always already there.

Her raven hair
Filled the sky
As her substance eased
Into being toward Truth.

She had
A fundamental trust
In the way
The Truth and the life
That guided her to freedom
And the chains of the world
Could not hold her down.

When she landed
In the domain of pure music
The deep touch stirred
The peace beyond understanding
Into her heart.

Then
Light returned to her third eye.

Then
She breathed in
Cosmic consciousness.

Then
The will
Of The Unknown God
Equipped her for battle
In the war of principalities.

It was
Her birth into being Lady Liberty.

Then
She called upon the patriots
Across the land to take a stand
Against the puppet masters.

So
It was time
To serve and protect
The home of the free and the brave.

*

While in trance
Eagle Hawk envisioned
The doctrine
Of the landscape
Roaring in the minds
Of the children of promise
As it buried Lady Liberty
And darkness consumed
Freedom.

Leaving the shadows
Of hatred
The power mongers poured
Their venom
Across the land
Of milk and honey
As they burned
The stars and stripes.

So
It was as time
When they lynched Truth
With the strings
Of the puppet masters
As they silenced
The voice of freedom
By ripping out the tongue
Of the way
The Truth and the life.

So
It was a time
Of double speak
When deception ruled.

Among the children
Of promise
Rose an army of patriots
And they pulled
Lady Liberty from the grave
As The Unknown God
Restored her breath
Of life.

Then
The patriots assembled
Armed and ready
To fight the good fight
With the courage
That would not surrender
To defeat.

So
It was the war
Of principalities.

Then
Eagle Hawk pulled
Out of trance
Shaken by his vision
Thankful
That The Spirit of Wisdom
Ruled.

*

Filling the moment
Pure music traces
The mystery of life
Into being toward Truth
As Annabelle Lee stands
At the edge of mind
Where thought leaps
Into endless possibility.

Opening her third eye
To a parabola of time
She witnesses time present
Dangling from a white oak tree
As the puppet masters
Driver nails into the hands
Of what matters.

Then
Pure music bleeds
Into her heart
As hidden meaning
Leads her to blind want.

Then
The sky opens to the secrets
Of time and space.

There is
Pain in this
Existential moment
That takes Annabelle Lee
Into the tombs of doubt
As the thunder
Of always already there
Awakens the dead.

Seeing through a looking glass
She rides on a thought
Across a wasteland
Where power mongers cripple
Free spirits.

Then
The children of promise
Advance into the here and now
Carrying the banner of the way
The Truth and the life
As pure music trumpets
The rise of the patriots.

Armed with The Spirit of Wisdom
They follow Lady Liberty into the glory
Of The Unknown God.

*

In the garden
Of tables and chairs
The children of promise
Gathered and Annabelle Lee
Danced in the shadows
As she embraced the rhythm
Of cosmic consciousness.

Breaking into the light
She poured pure music
From her heart
And then she disappeared
In the sky.

The children of promise
Followed her
Into the dawn of thought
And the moment
Rubbed time into the no longer
As mind drifted
Through a channel
To endless possibility.

Then
Annabelle Lee joined
The celestial clocks
After harvesting Truth
From hidden meaning.

Through the deep touch
The Spirit of Wisdom
Guided her onto the way
The Truth and the life
And The Unknown God
Infused the children of promise
With bountiful hopes and dreams.

There was
An orchestration
Of being toward Truth
Into her substance.

There was
The eclipse of time and space
By her dance.

Returning
To the garden
Of tables and chairs
Annabelle Lee planted thought
As a witness to Truth.

Then
Mind rested in the vision
Of the always already there.

So
Annabelle Lee carried on.

*

Traveling through the valley
Of dry bones
Following the flight
Of some crows
Annabelle Lee reached
Through her third eye
To catch a glimpse
Of a dangling man
With pure music
Bleeding from his heart.

As the drums of eternity
Rolled thunder
From the beyond
Her meditation took her
To the way
The Truth and the life
And the deep touch
Mounted her mind
Upon the always
Already there.

There was
The spark of thought
As she pulled the trigger
On being toward Truth
And the valley
Of dry bones danced
Into life.

So
Annabelle Lee
From a kingdom by the sea
Opened the graves
Of time past
And the children of promise
Gathered in pools of tears.

Suddenly
The other side of the sky
Poured being and nothingness
Into times and a half
And The Spirit of Wisdom
Kissed her cheek.

Then
Hidden meaning wrote Truth
Into the hearts
Of the children of promise
Those who grew
Out of the dry bones
And the dangling man
Whispered life
Into Annabelle Lee's ear.

Then
She launched her vision
Into the peace
Beyond understanding.

*

As the rhythm
Of pure music
Infuses the deep touch
Into being toward Truth
Annabelle Lee leaps
Into the unknown
In pursuit
Of the authentic article.

Trusting in the integrity
Of cosmic consciousness
She travels
Beyond time and space
To a river of thought
In a wilderness
Of endless possibility.

As she looks
Into the reflection
Of the waters
Clouds surround
The existential moment
And she faces the abyss.

It was
The naked pain
Of being and nothingness
That she felt
As the mask of denial
Smothered the breath
Of thought.

Gasping for life
She reached into blind want
With a passion
For Truth
As hidden meaning painted
The silhouette of trust
With the blood
Of the no longer.

Then
The bells of eternity
Tolled over the grave
Of Truth
And Annabelle Lee wept.

Then
Silence crushed hope
As darkness disfigured
Times and a half.

When Annabelle Lee heard
Pure music echo
Across her mind, she climbed out
Of her pain, and followed a portal
To what matters
Restoring being toward Truth.

So
Her trek across the unknown
Testified to the indwelling
Of the authentic article
In her life.

*

In the wilds of darkness
Where time past hides
Mind spins in erasure
And the war
Of principalities festers
In silence.

As the vision
In the looking glass
Bleeds into time present
An old man stumbles
Across the back roads
Of being and nothingness.

Dwelling in his affliction
He buries his mind
In the no longer
As his will to be
Drains into the abyss.

He has learned to suffer alone.

At the edge of eternity
He listens to the ache
In his bones
As time passes him
Into the void.

Then
Time future dies.

So
The old man
Has experienced
Out living self.

From the pit
Of his desolation
He looks
Through the window
Of the way
The Truth and the life
And he finds
Deliverance into hope.

Then
His crippled mind
Dances
To pure music
And he sees
The mystery of life
As a calling
To being toward Truth.

Awakened
To the presence
Of The Unknown God
The old man
Writes his destiny
Into the starry night.

Then
The Spirit of Wisdom
Kisses his cheek.

*

Catching the wind
In the sails
Of being toward Truth
Her voyage traverses
Time and space
As her mind opens
Her third eye
To cosmic consciousness.

In the moment
When the seas
Give up the dead
Annabelle Lee sinks
Into trance
And waves of thought
Drown
In endless possibility.

Then
What matters
Takes her
Into a parabola of time
And visions
Of pure music guide her
Through the unknown.

It is
The birth of eternity
In the here and now
That calls her
Onto the shores
Of the mystery of life.

So
The deep touch
Of being and nothingness
Stirs images
Of hidden meaning
Behind the mask
Of self-deception.

Following echoes
Of pure music
Annabelle Lee fathoms
The waters
Of the authentic article
As she dives further
Into the unknown.

It was
That being toward Truth
Painted her voyage
Into memories
As time past pictured
Cosmic consciousness
Upon her mind.

Then
Darkness disappeared.

Then
The light of forevermore
Awakened thought.

So
Her voyage took her
Behind the mask
Of the mystery of life.

*

When she looks
Into his hazel eyes
The mystery of life
Unfolds in a language
Formed by the deep touch
And pure music flows
Through the moment
That they share.

As they unite in a journey
Through a looking glass
Time present melts
Into the always already there
And passion sweats
In their heat.

As they climb
Into each other's mind
Whole worlds explode
Into the colors
Of forevermore
And the drums of eternity
Nest in their throbbing hearts.

So
Annabelle Lee embraces
The gift of his presence
As he echoes
Throughout her substance.

So
He cherishes
The treasures of her ways
And he is there
To serve and protect
All that she is.

Together
He and Annabelle Lee
March into the war
Of principalities
Their courage a testament
To what matters.

Their destiny
Is to triumph
Over tyranny
And free those
Under oppression.

It is
That victory flows
Through their veins.

So
The bond
Between Lady Liberty
And The Unknown Soldier
Defines
An immutable force.

*

The day before the kiss
Of darkness
Shadows swallowed
An old man
As he captured hidden meaning
And thoughts crawled
Into a bedroom of broken glass.

Leaving time and space
He rode upon liquid thunder
As the shadows gave him up
To outliving self
And the here and now
Drained his blood.

There was
The stir of madness
In the moment
As mind floundered
In the shadows
And the old man
Witnessed the collapse
Of times and a half.

Then
Eternity whispered
In his ear
And visions
Of being and nothingness
Hung in silence.

As the old man stepped
Through a looking glass
Into endless possibility
The given
Dressed his heart
With the authentic article.

Then
He released hidden meaning
Into the dawn
Of being toward Truth.

Then
The always already there
Formed his substance
Into echoes of Truth
As he traveled
Through the eye
Of a needle.

Then
Pure music embraced him
With the deep touch.

So
The old man dodged
The shadows
And cancelled the kiss
Of darkness
As he breathed in the breath
Of cosmic consciousness.

*

From deep in the abys
He searched
Through a looking glass
For the way
The Truth and the life
When his want
Blinded his vision.

There was
The shattering of time
And space
As he pulled images
From the deep touch
Of The Unknown God
And he mounted
His engine of thunder.

Wheeling through his pain
He connected
To the other side of time
As his mind spun
Into the workings
Of the celestial clocks.

Then
He painted the earth
Of being and nothingness
Reflected
In a parabola of time
And a figure of desire
Stood at the threshold
Of pure music.

So
He is an artist
Configuring a message
From his heart
As thoughts color
The authentic article
With the blood
Of forevermore.

Then
He breathes in
The Spirit of Wisdom
As the dull round
Triggers an ache
For being toward Truth.

Pyramiding through
The looking glass
He trumpets
The mystery of life
With the rhythm
Of the always already there
And his substance
Removes the mask
Of his vision.

So
He gathers the remains
Of time and space
Into an epiphany
Of deliverance
Through the abyss.

*

Running in circles
Mind hungers for Truth
As the heart drives time
Into a void
And being and nothingness
Outlives self.

There is
A passageway somewhere
Out of this dark pit
But the here and now
Stumbles into a blind vision.

As the pitch eats thought
Breathing heaves ashes
Of the no longer
And the odor of death
Surrounds this interlude
Of devastation.

So
It is the death
Of hope
That crushes time present
And life lies down
In a shallow grave.

In the nakedness of distress
The mask of the lost
Burns in the hollows
Of the eyes
And time stops.

Suddenly
Pure music writes images
Of the beyond
Onto her look
And castles of sand
Rise from the sea
Into fortresses of the will
To be.

So
She lifts her vision
Onto the way
The Truth and the life
As her third eye
Follows traces
Of The Spirit of Wisdom.

Then
The here and now
Finds her
As being toward Truth
And she bathes in the light
Of The Unknown God.

How
Her faith is
The passageway
Out of darkness.

*

SECTION 6:
Walking in pure music

As forevermore dissolves
In time and times and a half
The war of principalities
Grabs the here and now
By the throat
And Lady Liberty pulls
The trigger on fake news.

So
Truth hides in pockets
Of the forgotten
And the dull round
Cripples free spirits.

As darkness consumes
The beacon of hope
The children of promise
Assemble in the valley
Of dry bones
Armed with the way
The Truth and the life.

So
Lady Liberty rises
From the dust of minds
And the blood of patriots
Flows through
The back roads and alley ways,

Then
Being toward Truth awakens.

There is
Thunder in the belly
Of times and a half
And Lady Liberty wields
Lightning
With power and might.

Since the breath of freedom
Lives in the presence
Of The Unknown God
The patriots stand their ground
And the power mongers
Cry out for mercy.

Guided by The Spirit of Wisdom
Lady Liberty takes back
The home of the free and the brave
As the puppet masters
Devour themselves with their greed.

So
Lady Liberty restored life
To times and a half
And the free and brave
Trumpeted being toward Truth.

*

When time wrecked
On the shores
Of being and nothingness
And the shadows
Of outliving self
Smothered life, liberty
And the pursuit of happiness
Being toward Truth reached
Into waves of pure music
And the anthem
Of forevermore marched
Into the war of principalities.

While time present
Sunk in sewers
Of thought control
Lady Liberty gathered
The children of promise
Into troupes of patriots
Armed and ready to fight
For freedom.

It was
The destiny
Of being toward Truth
To harvest the times
Into a more perfect union
As Lady Liberty
Uprooted the deception
Of power mongers.

So
The battleground
Of the current revolution
Weighed heavily
Upon the hearts and minds
Of the children of promise
As the puppet masters
Saw to it
That the stars and stripes
Burned alive.

Then
The sun rose across a nation.

Then
The light of forevermore dawned.

So
The dull round crashed
Into times and a half
And Lady Liberty
Waved the banner
Of Truth and justice.

Then
Being toward Truth restored
A nation to the way
The Truth and the life
As pure music trumpeted
From sea to shining sea.

*

In the center
Of time and space
Pure music pulls the trigger
On a starry night
When mind eclipses
Being and nothingness.

As the landscape
Of the deep touch
Reveals the dawn
Breaking across mind
A moment appears
In the looking glass
Of the third eye
And thoughts echo
Across the terrain.

Then
Being toward Truth
Allows the artist
To picture
The other side
Of time present
As the trumpets of the always
Already there punctuate
The message
From the mystery of life.

Then
The muse dances
Across the horizon
Dressed in hidden meaning.

So
Pure music liberates
The moment
From the here and now.

Then
The artist in the form
Of another life
Traced the image
Of a dangling man
As heart defined
What matters.

Walking through the history
Written on stone tablets
The muse opened
The third eye to the way
The Truth and the life.

Then
Time and space declared
The ends of the unknown
And the artist carved
Being toward Truth
Into forevermore.

It was
The Spirit of Wisdom
That guided a witness
To The Unknown God
Through the deep touch
Of the artist.

*

As being toward Truth
Approached
Cosmic consciousness
The authentic article
Raised the substance
Of the existential moment
Into the always
Already there and clouds
Of hidden meaning vanished
From times and a half.

There were
Traces of the mystery of life
Embedded
Into the here and now
And Annabelle Lee formed them
Into an apothecary of thought.

As her mind heeled
From her wounds in the battles
In the war of principalities
She opened her third eye
To pure music
And time present articulated
What was there
Behind the mask
Of being and nothingness.

So
The authentic article
Strengthened her bond
To forevermore.

It was
Her trust in cosmic
Consciousness
That brought the vision
Of the existential moment.

It was
Times and a half
That brought her
To the edge of the abyss.

Then
The mystery of life
Pounded in her heart
As hidden meaning
Appeared
In the looking glass
Of time and space.

Then
Annabelle Lee emptied
Her mind in the cool
Of the abyss
As she warmed up
To pure music.

So
She thought herself
Beyond being and nothingness
And into the authentic
Article of cosmic consciousness.

*

It was
The voice of Lady Liberty
Penetrating hearts of darkness
That shook the world
As the children of promise
Gathered in the garden
Of tables and chairs.

Across the mountains
Those blue ridges
Freedom rose
As the blood of time
And times and a half
Drowned the puppet masters.

So
Lady Liberty carried
The destiny of free spirits
Into the dawn of forevermore
And the children of promise
Harvested Truth.

Then
The power mongers fell
Into the abyss
As they choked
On their deception.

It was
The union of free spirits
And the children of promise
That weaponized the patriots
In the war of principalities
As Lady Liberty
Undressed hidden meaning.

During this time
Cosmic consciousness equipped
The patriots with the power
Of pure music and the anthem
Of life, liberty and the pursuit
Of happiness conquered
The despots.

As Truth defined
The mystery of life
The voice of Lady Liberty
Triumphed
Over hearts of darkness
And the light of what matters
Showered freedom across the world.

Then
The puppet masters dangled
In the void.

Then
Being toward Truth dwelled
In the hearts and minds
In the garden
Of tables and chairs
And across the world.

*

When pure music showers
Upon times and a half
The echoes
Of being toward Truth
Wash upon the minds
Of those wandering
Through a wilderness of thought
And the mystery of life
Saturates yearning hearts.

When
Trance takes
To the hollow hours
Of the existential interlude
An old man
Reaches the home
Of being and nothingness
Through a parabola of time.

During this moment
Centered upon the here
And now
He uncovers the graves
Of thought
And his mind awakens
To forevermore.

Then
The drums of eternity
Thunder
Through the back roads
Of mind.

How
The old man pyramids
Into a two-dimensional
Reality
And the silhouette
Of yearning hearts
Follow him
Through a portal
To the authentic article.

Then
The wilderness of thought
Howls
As he pursues hidden meaning.

Then
Pure music pours Truth
Into times and a half
And the old man
ventures into the other side
Of the sky
As cosmic consciousness
Forms a one-dimensional
Reality in his mind.

It is
That he dwells
In being toward Truth
Calling to those
Wandering through thought.

*

Waiting in the chambers
Of the beyond
Counting the teeth
In the night
Mind stirs in the presence
Of the celestial clocks
As destiny
Uncovers possibility.

As the clouds
Of the here and now
Leave footprints
In thoughts
Memories move
Shadows in the darkness.

So
Eagle Hawk climbs
Out of self
And the drums
Of eternity
Drive his life
Into nonbeing.

Then
A crystal blue
Shines into his third eye
As he feels the passion
Of being toward Truth.

Then
He hears Annabelle Lee
Cary a song.

Crashing through the walls
Of the beyond
They paint the empty hands
Of hunger
As the children of promise
Throw their hearts
After critical needs.

How
The hungry moments
Pyramid life
Into the skeleton
Of time and space
As Eagle Hawk and Annabelle Lee
Kiss the feet
Of cosmic consciousness.

As nonbeing liberates them
From the solitary confinement
Of the here and now
The always already there
Empties the mystery of life
Into the celestial clocks.

So
The waiting was over.

So
Eagle Hawk and Annabelle Lee
Traveled together onto forevermore
Followed by the children of promise.

*

It was
A time to gather
The songs
That move the mind
Beyond horizons
Of thought
Through images stirring
In the third eye.

Believing self into the muscle
Of being toward Truth
The artist launched his trance
Into endless possibility
And pure music surrounded him
With the passion of the quick.

Echoing across the landscape
Of being and nothingness
The voices of eternity carried
The mystery of life
Into the heart of what matters
And the artist
Formed the moment
That reached the deep touch.

Then
Cosmic consciousness lifted
His vision
Onto the always already there.

Then
A portal to a one
Dimensional reality
Pulled him from the shadows
Of the dull round
As the center
Of a fearless symmetry
Painted songs in the mind.

So
The image
Of being toward Truth
Opened his third eye
To horizons
Beyond time and space
As the warm of pure music
Covered the artist with love.

Witnessing The Spirit of Wisdom
The artist painted
Oracles of Truth
As songs of the times
Unearthed hidden meaning.

So
The artist removed the mask
Of the existential moment
Revealing the heartbeat
Of forevermore.

*

As pure music carries
The mind into visions
Of The Spirit of Wisdom
The dull round pushes
Thoughts into caves
Of darkness.

It is
A struggle to look
Beyond the pain
Piercing mind.

To think
Outside the here and now
When an ache breaks bones
She seeks the peace
Beyond understand.

Then
Time and space crumbled
But the blood of Truth
Voided
The existential moment.

There was
A stillness in the air.

There was
The slaughter
In time and space.

When drums of eternity
Thundered
Across the way
The Spirit of Wisdom
Took the look
Of Annabelle Lee
Into what matters.

As the darkness
Dissolved in pools of light
Visions of being toward Truth
Sparked thoughts
From the unknown
And trumpets
Of forevermore signaled
The moment to be.

Then
She rode pure music
With the breath
Of The Spirit of Wisdom.

So
She conquered her turmoil
With the way, the Truth
And the life.

*

As The Spirit of Wisdom
Countered the darkness
With dreams and hope
Time slipped into a reckoning
And the children of promise
Turned to the way
The Truth and the life.

Following pure music
Into the dawn of possibility
They severed their ties
To the dull round
And climbed
Into being toward Truth.

There was
A chill to the bones
When the darkness raged.

There was
Destiny written
Upon tablets of stone.

So
Each day they stepped
Into the unknown
With visions of The Word
As they read hidden meaning
Between the lines
Of forevermore.

Facing the rhetoric
Of the puppet masters
The children of promise
Erased the language
Of deception
As The Unknown God
Spoke to their hearts
And they accepted
The mystery of life
As the always already there.

Then
A one-dimensional reality
Encompassed them
With a brilliant light
That canceled the shadows
Of the existential moment.

There is
The beginning of forevermore
In the lives
Of the children of promise.

There is
The certainty of Truth
In their minds.

Orchestrating the times
The Spirit of Wisdom
Allowed them life
Liberty and the pursuit
Of happiness.

*

In the twilight hours
When stillness covers
The earth
And the push
Into silence aligns
Time and space
With dreams
The children of promise
Search the unknown
For pure music.

Finding what matters
They drink in
The deep touch
That restores life
Into the living moment
As time present
Seeps into the rhythm
Of the drums of eternity.

Then
The starry night
Comforts them
With whispers of love
And the majesty
Of The Unknown God
Embraces them with Truth.

Drifting into the always
Already there
They accept deliverance
Into the peace
Beyond understanding.

As they hunger
For the way
The Truth and the life
The children of promise
Reach for the celestial clocks
For a sign of the times
And the shadows
Of the dull round
Dribble into the no longer.

So
They connect
To The Spirit of Wisdom.

So
They feel the power
Of cosmic consciousness.

Then
A silhouette of their thoughts
Carries them into visions.

There is
The dance
Into the mystery of life.

Although the world retreats
Into chaos
Pure music secures
The faith
Of the children of promise.

None is lost.

*

Speaking in blood
Eagle Hawk colored
The world with hope
And the children of promise
Caught the rhythm
Of his tongue.

It was
A language undressing
Hidden meaning
And removing the mask
Of the here and now.

As he walked
Through volumes of thought
The children of promised
Felt the deep touch
Of The Spirit of Wisdom.

They gathered the will
To journey
Into the unknown
And the back roads
Of mind
As Eagle Hawk pointed
To the way
The Truth and the life.

Then
Being toward Truth
Formed the substantial
In their substance.

There were
Songs in their hearts
That liberated them
From the inhibitions
Fostered by the dull round.

Suddenly
They were surrounded
By pure music.

Then
Visions of the dawn
Of forevermore swept
Across the horizon
And Eagle Hawk wrote
The commands
Of The Unknown God
On tablets of stone.

As time and times
And a half registered
Truth in their hearts
Eagle Hawk led them
Through the wilderness
To the promised land.

So
Eagle Hawk echoed
The destiny
Of the children of promise.

*

It was
Her will to be
That conquered oppression
As Lady Liberty waved
The banner of Truth
And justice
And she sang an anthem
Of freedom
Across the land.

As she walked
Through the shallow graves
Of the fallen
Her tears numbered
The dreams
Of the children of promise.

Facing the darkness
Of the despots
She brought the light
Of The Spirit of Wisdom
And the shadows
Of deceit
Retreated into a chasm
Of the no longer.

There was
The cry of the lives
Who fought deception
With the child of mountains
And the way
The Truth and the life
Triumphed.

Then
Lady Liberty trumpeted
The victory of Truth.

Then
The children of promise
Rose into the light
Of forevermore.

As the dull round
Awoke from the absurd
The madness
Of being and nothingness
Decayed.

So
She dwelt in the presence
Of The Unknown God
Onto eternity
And the children of promise
Celebrated the return
Of Truth and justice.

*

So
It was existential thought
Founded upon absurdity
That brought him down
Into the pit of despair
As he grieved cover a lack
Of purpose.

Feeding on sour grapes
Groveling
In pointlessness
He witnessed the collapse
Of the universe
As he stepped
Ever closer to the no longer.

There was
No dawn to his nightmare.

There was
The interminable darkness
Only.

Wallowing in self pity
He shredded his heart
Into stillness
As his dirge advanced
His life into the void
As he choked on his words.

Claiming ownership
Of the authentic article
Because he was among the lost
He prided himself
As confronting the abyss
Until his vague advanced
Onto a starry night.

Then
He saw the other side
Of being and nothingness.

Then
He grasped his purpose
By connecting
To beauty and Truth.

It was
His birth into pure music
That took his mind
Into celestial dynasties
And then unto a one
Dimensional reality.

Shedding the skin
Of despair, he fed
On the Spirit of Wisdom
That carried him to the way
The Truth and the life,

As he witnessed
Truth and beauty
He trumpeted pure music
Onto the dawn of life.

*

Once again
Traveling beyond time and space
He expanded his vision
'through his third eye
To explore the domain
Of the always already there.

As he throttled
Into the unknown
Leaving the here and now
He projected himself
Into being toward Truth
And the light of forevermore
Shone upon him.

Then
Tears of gold flooded
The moment with thoughts.

Then
From the hollows
Of an existential interlude
Hidden meaning erased
The sky,

A void encompassed all
And everything.

As time and times
And a half unfolded
Into the quick
Of being and nothingness
His mind stopped.

Then
A song drove the engine
Of his will.

Then
He felt the chill
Of the no longer
Grip him with jaws
Of gravity.

Then
Pure music carried his form
Onto the engine of The unknown God
Through cosmic consciousness
As the drums of eternity
Marched into his mind

There was
The rebirth of thought
That wove the moment
Into a one-dimensional reality.

The Word allowed him
To awaken.

Before
When time died
He looked
To The Spirit of Wisdom
For the peace
Beyond understanding.

Suddenly
He felt the warm
Of the everlasting
Return to his mind.

*

SECTION 7:
The blood of thought

When time tears holes
In the heart
And space dies in darkness
Mind turns to the rhythm
Of the universe
The pure music
Of the everlasting
And the devotion
Of The Unknown God.

There is
Pain lingering
In the shadows
As a crippled mind
Drags itself through the blood
Of the here and now
Until the deep touch
Of The Word delivers
The peace
Beyond understanding.

Then
The heart celebrates
The dawn of hope.

Then
The mind dances
After being released
From the bondage
Of suffering.

Then
She sees the way
The Truth and the life
In a looking glass
As the warm
Of cosmic consciousness
Encompasses
The here and now.

So
Annabelle Lee found a way
Through the existential interlude
As the expanse weighed
Upon her heart
And the dull round
Hungered for her life.

Then
She dined
On The Spirit of Wisdom.

Then
Time and space dawned
An age of hope
As visions surfaced.

Believing herself
Beyond the moment
Of collapse
Her third eye traced
Eternity to a house
Of many mansions.

So
Annabelle Lee followed
A song into paradise.

*

Through pure music
She encompassed thoughts
Far beyond the here and now
As the rhythm
Pounded by the drums
Of eternity
Drove being toward Truth
Onto the mystery of life.

In her eyes shone
The Spirit of Wisdom
And she wore
The face of beauty.

Her tongue formed a message
Of the everlasting
As time and times
And a half followed her
Onto forevermore.

When she sang
Her voice signified
The flight of a free spirit.

Rising from the ashes
Of a burned-out world
She summoned the after glow
Of hidden meaning
As the night
Tip-toed treasures
Of dreams.

Then
He saw her
In a meadow of daffodils
The perfume of pure music
Sweeping him
Into the stars.

Following the moon
Into her sweet embrace
He gathered kisses
Of cosmic consciousness
As the elements of mind
Worked their way
Into the always
Already there.

Then
The sky opened
His trance
To The Book of Life
As the pages colored
The moment with hope
And together
The grew into a mountain
Of Truth.

Through their faith
In The Unknown God
They launched into a one
Dimensional reality
And the light
Of forevermore delivered them
Into pure music.

*

When the magic
Of the underworld works
Through time and space
Life is filled with darkness
And Annabelle Lee speaks
A way through the treachery.

There is
The silence
Of a stillborn world
Bathed in the ashes
Of deception and time spins
A web of lies.

Although the spells
Cast from the graves
Of deceit bury Truth
In the muscle of things
In themselves
She dresses in the light
Of the way
The Truth and the life.

Then
The mystery of life
Masks hidden meaning
And the face
Of the always already there
Appears in the looking glass.

Although torrents of destruction
Ruin the moment
She walks through the walls
Of magic
As she targets
The the-slight-of-mind.

There is
Release from the solitary
Confinement of mind
As she searches
For The Spirit of Wisdom.

Then
The Word
Recovers Annabelle Lee
From the darkness
As she reads
Between the lines
Of hidden meaning
With her third eye.

So
Her journey
Into the abyss
Taught her being
Toward Truth
In the tongue
Of forevermore
As The Unknown God
Defined pure music
In her heart.

*

Headed down the road blind
The sky collapsing
And stars scattering
Across the pavement
The artist witnesses
The dawn of destruction
Through his third eye.

Across the way
The wilderness marches
Closer
As the trees ignite
In wild flames.

Drawing near
The flora blazes
And the fauna screams
In the inferno.

There is
The trumpet of life
Sounding the charge
Of chaos
And the world
Bleeds into the tracks
Of the no longer.

So
The artist addresses
The doom of the dull round
As time infuses
The moment with dread.

Searching for hope
He stumbles upon the deep touch
Of the Unknown God
And times change.

Then
The destiny of the world
Writes pure music
Into the heart
And the artist steps
Into the call of nonbeing.

Believing himself
Into being toward Truth
He envisions pure music
And The Spirit of Wisdom
Releases the way
The Truth and the life
Into free spirits.

Although the war
Of principalities
Chars the authentic article
The artist pyramids
The mystery of life
Into the breath
Of forevermore
And he rises
From his ashes.

*

When being toward Truth
Summoned the stars, the moon
And the earth
Into the always already there
The authentic article
Of being and nothingness took
To the way, the Truth
And the life.

There was
The echo of chaos
Wafting across time and space
As lungs emptied
Their wind into the void.

So
It was troubled times
That betrayed Lady Liberty
As powermongers ate
The lives of the children
Of promise.

It was
Th cruelty
Of the puppet masters
That obliterated
The thoughts of free spirits
But a remnant wrote
Their lives
With Lady Liberty.

They were
The underground
Serving The Spirit of Wisdom
Holding certain Truths
As self-evident.

They prospered in the shadows
Of the dull round
And they flourished with the blood
Of Truth.

So
The despots trembled
Before The Unknown God
As they were stricken
By their own poison.

It was
The courage
Of the children of promise
That fed minds
With the treasures
Of forevermore.

So
Lady Liberty triumphs
Over agents of decadence
As she slays
The monsters of time
And space.

*

The drama of the moment
Rubs coarse over thoughts
When the moon turned to blood
And shadows covered
The mind with trembling.

Appearing out of darkness
An old man shuffles
Across the stage
As the actors fall
Through time and space
And hope hangs
From a banyan tree.

There is
A nervous silence to the crowd
As waves of pain
Scour them with grief.

It is
All about the powermongers
And their will to silence
The hearts of the audience.

So
The winds of time
And times and a half
Smothered the moment
Until the third act
Murdered Truth.

Then
The curtain fell
And the old man
Scattered the bones
Of the witnesses.

There was
No life to the moment
As he picked his way
Through the rubble.

There was
The melody of the macabre
As he bled across the graves
Of the forgotten.

Then
The powermongers
Applauded him
Throwing flowers
And hand grenades
At his feet.

Balancing
Being and nothingness
In his mind
The old man wove
A fiction of betrayal
Onto the survivors
And they thought it
A passage
Of hidden meaning.

Exiting the moment
The children of promise
Equipped their passion.

*

As pure music delivers
The authentic article
Into being toward Truth
Annabelle Lee dances
Into the heart of the artist
And the moment breeds
The deep touch.

It is an awakening
To the mystery of life.

It is
The traveling of mind
Beyond time and space.

Then
The artist liberates
The unknown from the magic
Of being and nothingness
And Annabelle Lee
Speaks Truth
Into the shadows
Where images portray
The life of pure music.

Clearing the moment
The artist knifes the heart.

So
Annabelle Lee emerged
Through a looking glass
As the artist pulled Truth
From what matters
And they leaped
Into cosmic consciousness.

Together
They defined the sweet
Scent of love
And the opening
Of the unknown
To the third eye.

So
The children of promise
Feasted upon the riches
Of the moment
Connecting to the dance
Of possibility and the artist
Carried Annabelle Lee
In his heart
Onto the always
Already there.

Then
Being toward Truth
Dwells with the deep touch.

*

Traveling far beyond
The here and now
She eclipsed being
And nothingness
As the existential moment
Stretched her trance
Into endless possibility.

Surrounded by pure music
She felt the deep touch
Of the authentic article
As the mystery of life
Connected her to Truth
And the shadows
Of time past dissolved
In the light of the always
Already there.

Then
Her trance took her
Through a looking glass.

Then
Her mind dwelt
With being toward Truth.

There is
A touchstone
For a free spirit
In her trance that allows her
To feel the light
Of forevermore
As she focuses upon the rhythm
Of the universe.

There was
The roll of drums
Of eternity echoing
In caverns of her thought.

There was
The image of being
And nothingness
Dangling from a banyan tree
As the dread of being there
Turned to the peace
Beyond understanding.

Then
She felt the power
Of pure music
Come upon her
As she muscled her way
Through the looking glass
Of what matters.

Although time and space
Clutter the mind
With trepidation
The mask of dread
Leaves her face
Of nonbeing unmarred.

*

Echoes of the universe
Drift into mind
As thoughts travel
Into the substance
Of hidden meaning.

There is
A tight fit
Of phenomenal reality
Over being toward Truth
As cosmic consciousness
Unearths being and nothingness.

Believing self into nonbeing
Annabelle Lee configures
Time and space
Into pure music
As the universe articulates
The mystery of life
Into the moment
When Truth speaks
To the heart.

Climbing mountains
To touch the sky
She grasps the beyond
As entrance into the always
Already there.

Then
She appears
In a one-dimensional reality.

Then
A vertical column of time
Delivers her from dread
And life awakens
To images of the deep touch.

When she expands herself
Into hidden meaning
The breath of nonbeing
Liberates her
From the solitary confinement
Of the dull round
As being toward Truth
Opens thought
To the other side
Of time and space.

It is
The return of hope
To the children of promise
That muscles
Annabelle Lee into the image
Of Lady Liberty
Because freedom speaks
Louder than words.

Then
She rides times and a half
Across the universe
Through the looking glass
Of nonbeing.

*

Purging herself
From being and nothingness
Annabelle Lee launches
Into the expanse
As her meditation takes her
Into the heart
Of cosmic consciousness.

There is
The rhythm of pure music
Liberating her
From the constraints
Of the dull round
As she ventures
Through a looking glass.

Then
She feels the deep touch
Of The Spirit of Wisdom.

Then
The way
The Truth and the life
Cleanses her
Form and substance.

Then
The Unknown God
Opens the door
To the house
Of many mansions
And forevermore
Is her destiny.

Above the clouds
And far beyond the sky
Her meditation carries her
Into the muscle
Of being toward Truth
As a vertical column of time
Witnesses her dance
Across time and space.

Although she struggled
With the absurdity
Of the puppet masters
Annabelle Lee attached herself
To pure music
And the drums of eternity
Paraded her into the peace
Beyond understanding.

Then
The children of promise
Proved victorious
Over the despots.

Then
She felt the freedom
Of Lady Liberty.

Then
The fullness of time returned.

*

Trusting in The Spirit of Wisdom
The old man gathered
His bones and headed out
To find the good shepherd
As the darkness
Of the despots covered
The here and now.

There was
The pounding of a false narrative
That drove Truth into hiding.

When the old man
Opened his mind
To pure music
Cosmic consciousness
Shone brilliance upon him.

Because he left the absurdity
Of the existential moment
That tried
To confound him
His third eye connected
To the glory
Of The Unknown God.

So
The old man followed Truth
Through the shadows
Of deception
Cast by the dull round
Until the graves
Gave up their dead
And an awakening
Shattered the agendas
Of the puppet masters.

Then
Lady Liberty embraced
His heart
Because his mind sought
Refuge from the storm.

Sitting beneath a banyan tree
He listens to the call of Lady Liberty
As pure music accompanies her
Into his mind.

Then
He sees the good shepherd
Come down from the heavens
And The Spirit of Wisdom
Infuses within him
Being toward Truth.

So
The old man's name
Is written
In The Book of Life
Because he follows
The way
The Truth and the life.

*

There is
A voyage to the unknown
Taken by the artist
As his mask portrays brilliance
While the existential moment
Smothers his face.

With a heaving breath
He wanders from image to image
Trapped by the void
And haunted
By a vicious muse.

Giving his blood for an idea
His heart rages in his chest
As he seeks Truth.

Buried in hidden meaning
The artist unearths The Stary Night
While his mind sinks
Into a sea of pain.

While he cruises
Through time and space
Madness fuels his passion
As he dissolves in hard times.

The melody of madness
Leads his deep touch
Into the always
Already there.

Radiating through his bones
An echo cripples his vision
As he feels his way
Across the expanse.

Then
A lone lark bucks
The wind across a golden field
And the harvest
Of his soul gathers nothingness.

Plunging a dagger
Through his spine
His muse covers his body
With thorns
As rats gnaw on his toes.

There is
A Truth only revealed through struggle.

Although the artist
Bleeds in the dark cold
He wills himself
To endure.

There is
An island of refuge
In his seething sea
Of madness
And it is the triumph
Of his work
Hidden from his life.

*

Beyond the clouds
Of times and a half
Mind dances
As the mystery of life
Comes out from the shadows.

There is
The echo of pure music
Lifting thoughts
Into another dawn
From the always
Already there.

Following the rhythm
Of the deep touch
She reaches
Into hidden meaning.

Then
The crystal images
Through the looking glass
Unmask the face
Of being and nothingness.

There is
The pounding of drums
Driving her
Beyond the existential moment
As the mystical
Dresses her
In the light of forevermore.

As the mystery of life
She dances
Through a portal
To the other side
Of time and space
Where trumpets of stone
Salute her passage
Into pure music.

Then
Being toward Truth
Awakens her substance.

Then
The Spirit of Wisdom
Takes her thoughts
Beyond being and time.

Then
The clouds of hidden meaning
Disappear
And she celebrates
The presence of the way
The Truth and the life
In her heart.

After all and everything
She dances in the presence
Of The Unknown God.

*

Through meditation she feels
The deep touch of splendor
From The Unknown God
As her mind loads pure music.

Leaving behind the trappings
Of the dull round
She mounts beams of light
And heads out
For the mystery of life.

Between beats of her heart
She registers hidden meaning
From the unknown
As a two-dimensional reality
Pictures the landscape of mind
Through a looking glass
In the-close-at-hand.

It is
The wonder
From The Spirit of Wisdom
That carries her from the dread
Of existential times
To the way, The Truth and the life
As she unmasks
Being and nothingness.

Then
Visions stirring her thoughts
Picture being toward Truth
And the drums of eternity
Lead her
Through a parabola of time.

So
It is that The Spirit of Wisdom
Is the engine
Of The Unknown God
Pulling Truth
With cosmic consciousness
As the language of pure music.

Because pure music speaks her
Into the beyond, she recognizes
That the here and now
Passes away while Truth is
Of the always already there.

So
Liberating her
From linear time and space
A one-dimensional reality
Enlightens her
As she meditates her way
With the power of The Unknown God.

*

The dance of times
And a half filtered
Through the moonlight
Became the love
Of forevermore.

It was
That she lit the darkness
With brilliance in her eyes.

Her voice carried Truth
Into the moment
As pure music poured
From her heart.

As mind followed
The rhythm
Of the mystery of life
She wove a tapestry
Of songs in the sky.

Then
The moon colored the dance
Of being toward Truth
With blood.

It was
The sacrifice of the way
The Truth and the life
That redeemed time
As the always
Already there embraced
Thoughts
With The Spirit of Wisdom.

It was
That the morning light
Erased the moon
But the dance to eternity
Continued on.

Although shadows
Of being and nothingness
Targeted the children of promise
Lady Liberty faced
The existential moment
With the passion of pure music
As she read hidden meaning
From the clouds.

With the sun upon her back
She danced her way
Through the wall
Of blind hatred
Bringing the testament
Of the peace
Beyond understanding
From The Unknown God.

*

As her heart pounded
The debris of life
Into a wreckage
Of the human spirit
She held ever so tightly
To the image of hope
Cast through a looking glass.

As time and space
Plunged her
Into an existential moment
And the world canceled love
There was a doorway
In the expanse accessible
Through meditation.

Although an interlude
In the abyss trapped her
The Spirit of Wisdom
Embraced her
With pure music.

Then
The times heard her cry
From the wilderness
And they were armed
With the way, the Truth
And the life.

Then
Annabelle Lee rose
To bring love to the hatred.

It was
A war of principalities
Configuring the destiny
Of Truth.

It was
A struggle for Truth
That exploded
From sea to shining sea
As the tempest of the times
Raged in the heart.

Then
The dawn of it all
Flowered in the sky.

It was
The defeat of hatred
As Annabelle Lee led the charge
Of love into victory
As treasures of peace
Covered times and a half.

Then
The hatred died.

So
The power of love is greater
Than the power of hatred.

*

In the center of the abyss
Rages a storm
And he is there
Sweating in the heat
As torrents of wind
Crash thunder into mind.

As turmoil extends
Time into times and a half
He feels remote, dangling
In an existential moment.

Alone in the darkness
Naked in despair
His raw heart bleeds
On the cinder floor
Of desolation.

Although freedom he sought
He found his mind
In a cage of absurdity
As the world spun
Out of control.

His cry for mercy
Returned to him
Empty handed.

So
He marked his years
In the abyss
With his own blood
As the wind gusted
Dread in his heart.

Then
When the other side
Of time and space
Appeared to him
The peace
Beyond understanding
Liberated him
From being a victim.

It was
The love of The Unknown God
That embraced his festering heart.

Carrying him
To the house
Of many mansions
The Spirit of Wisdom
Dressed him
With wondrous thought.

Returning to his life
He willed himself
Into being toward Truth
And he stared down the abyss
Because the way
The Truth and the life
Filled him with the freedom
Of pure music.

So
He gives thanks
To The Unknown God.

*

As the free spirits
Made of muscle and mud
Looked into the star-lit night
They counted their steps
To eternity together
And they measured
The expanse
With a wink and nod.

There was
Pure music in their stand
As the moon covered them
With colors of wonder.

From their cradle of love
Rose the deep touch
Of forevermore
As a song embraced them
With the mystery of life.

To endure
The wilds of concrete
Where neon dribbles
The absurdity
Of existential moments
They mounted thunder
In the night.

Although time and space
Dissolve in dreams
Annabelle Lee reaches
Into the treasures
Of being toward Truth
As vapors of thought
Extend time
Into times and a half.

Then
She shapes a vision
Of the tickle
In the deep touch
And their sweat breeds
The children of promise
As trumpets announce
The dawn of another age.

As free spirits
They unearthed Truth
From the grave
Of being and nothingness
As they engaged
The rhythm of the universe.

Following the way
The Truth and the life
They had united
On their wedding night.

So
The children of promise
Are born again.

*

So
The world of double speak
Showers the mind
With darkness
As the ghost of Truth
Haunts the human heart.

It was
A time to bury faith
In the back room of thought.

So
They burned the books
Of pure music
And looted the treasures
Of history.

The writing on the wall
Was written in the blood
Of the children of promise
And despots hanged Lady Liberty
In the public square.

Although Truth nurtured
Minds for a while
The puppet masters
Canceled what is true
And the age
Of bondage began.

Locked out of life
The children of promise starved
In death camps
As the despots poured
venom
Into the minds
Of free spirits.

So
A remnant of Truth
Hid in the shadows
Carrying with them
The way
The Truth and the life.

Although the terror from the despots
Canceled freedom
A remnant endured by the will
Of The Spirit of Wisdom.

Although the slaughter
Of Truth extended
Across the dull round
The remnant went
Underground
Keeping the faith
In The Unknown God.

One day they will return
To the public square
Waving the banner
Of stars and stripes
With Truth and justice.

*

As pure music infuses
A right spirit
Into being toward Truth
The mystery of life dances
Across endless possibility
And the artist focuses
Upon hidden meaning.

Reaching beyond the here and now
His mind embraces the deep touch
As his meditation reveals
The essence
Of the always already there.

Then
Among the shadows
Of an existential moment
The ghosts
Of being and nothingness
Drag time into despair
As he looks
Through a wall of hatred.

Then
The experiential bleeds
The death
Of the dull round
Into the graveyard
Of forevermore.

Suspended in the fury
Of the moment
The artist opens
His heart
To a two-dimensional reality
As the mystery of life
Writes his name
With drops of blood
On the cave wall.

There is
The thread of forevermore
Weaving messages in the wind.

There is
Hope pulled by the trigger
Of pure music that delivers him
Through the pit of hatred
Onto treasures of Truth.

So

His meditation spans
The here and now
Onto the always already there
By his will to endure.

So

The Spirit of Wisdom
Saturated his substance
With the way
The Truth and the life
Onto the presence
Of The Unknown God.

*

To books by Dean C. Gardner, click
http://booksbydeancgardner.com